INSTRUCTIONAL DESIGN IS NOT ROCKET SCIENCE

ID MADE EASY

POOJA MALHOTRA

Contents

PREFACE

Learning has become a lifelong endeavour in today's fast-paced and knowledge-driven world. Organizations across various sectors recognize the importance of continuous learning to enhance employee performance, improve productivity, and foster innovation. As a result, the demand for skilled instructional designers and trainers has increased significantly.

This book is designed for professionals working in the field of education, instructional design, and training looking to expand their understanding of the key concepts. Freshers aspiring to become instructional designers and trainers and who are interested in understanding how people learn and how to formulate and deliver instruction will also find this book handy.

My endeavour here is to help you gain a comprehensive understanding of the implications of different learning theories, and practical strategies related to learning and instruction - with practical examples at every step of the way. You will explore various approaches to learning and examine their application in designing and delivering effective education in different contexts.

Throughout the book, you will delve into the foundations of how individuals acquire knowledge, develop skills, and change behaviours. This book will also enable you to examine the role of motivation, attention, memory, and metacognition in learning.

One of the critical focuses of this book is instructional design. You will gain insights into analyzing learning needs, setting clear objectives, and designing engaging and interactive learning experiences. You will explore different instructional methods and delivery formats and familiarize yourself with constructive strategies for facilitating collaborative learning, promoting active participation, and providing constructive feedback.

Whether you aim to work in corporate training, educational institutions, or any other learning-focused setting, this book will empower you to make a positive difference in your learners' lives.

Let's embark on this exciting journey into learning and instruction approaches and explore the fascinating field of instructional design.

I
Behaviourist School of Thought

The Behaviourist School of Thought in Psychology emphasizes the role of observable behaviour in learning and the relationship between stimuli and responses. According to behaviourists, learning results from conditioning, where individuals acquire new behaviours through associations between stimuli and responses.

In a groundbreaking experiment in the early 20th century, Russian physiologist Ivan Pavlov observed that dogs could associate the arrival of a technician with getting fed, causing them to salivate even before any food was present. This led Pavlov to uncover classical conditioning - a fundamental form of associative learning.

In contrast, B.F. Skinner's Operant Conditioning focused on voluntary responses to stimuli in the environment and showed that voluntary responses to stimuli could be reinforced or punished to shape behaviour. Skinner argued that the consequences following a specific behaviour can either increase or decrease that behaviour.

In 1963, Bandura and Walters introduced a new perspective on modeling behaviour, challenging the traditional idea of reinforcement through actions. Bandura later developed the social learning theory, which emphasizes the influence of significant individuals in a child's life, including parents, siblings, teachers, peers, and even television heroes.

Unlike the one-way impact of the environment on an individual, Bandura proposed reciprocal determinism, where personal factors, environmental factors, and behaviour all interconnect and influence each other. This theory acknowledges that conduct and environment are changeable and equally important in shaping behaviour.

For instance, aggressive children expect hostility from others, leading them to act aggressively, which then elicits more aggressive responses from others, reinforcing their initial expectations. On the other hand, children who respond in a friendly manner create a positive social environment.

The educational implications of behaviourist theories lie in their emphasis on external factors that influence learning outcomes. Some fundamental principles and examples of Behaviourist learning theories are:

Stimulus-Response (S-R) Theory

This theory suggests that learning occurs when a particular response follows a specific stimulus, leading to reinforcement. Instructional designers can use this principle by presenting clear and distinct stimuli to elicit desired responses. For example, in teaching a new language, providing audio prompts for learners to respond with correct pronunciation can reinforce the association between the stimulus (audio prompt) and the desired response (correct pronunciation).

Reinforcement and Rewards

Behaviourists emphasize using positive reinforcement and rewards to strengthen desired behaviours. Instructional designers can apply this principle to motivate learners by incorporating rewards, such as praise, grades, certificates, or tangible incentives. For instance, in an e-learning book, a system that provides badges or points for completing modules or achieving milestones can encourage learners to stay engaged and progress.

Shaping and Chaining

Behaviourists propose that people learn complex behaviours by splitting them into smaller, manageable steps. This process is known as shaping or chaining. Instructional designers can use this technique by designing instructional sequences that gradually build upon each other. For example, in teaching a complex software application, breaking it down into step-by-step tutorials that guide learners from basic to advanced features can facilitate their understanding and skill development.

Drill and Practice

Behaviourists advocate for repetitive practice to strengthen and reinforce learning. Instructional designers can incorporate drills and practice activities that allow learners to apply knowledge or skills repeatedly. For instance, in mathematics education, providing exercises with increasing difficulty levels and ample practice time will enable learners to reinforce their understanding of concepts and improve problem-solving skills.

Behaviour Modification

Behaviourist theories suggest that undesirable behaviours can be modified or replaced with desirable ones through positive and negative reinforcement, punishment, or extinction techniques. Behaviour modification techniques can be applied in learning and training by providing immediate feedback and consequences that promote desirable behaviours. For example, in workplace training for customer service, a simulated scenario highlighting the adverse effects of rude behaviour and rewarding positive interactions can help modify learner behaviours.

Examples

Below are some examples that demonstrate how behaviourist theories can effectively shape student behaviour in a classroom setting, creating an environment conducive to learning.

Positive reinforcement

Ms. Bhatti praises students and gives them stickers or extra playtime for completing assignments on time or demonstrating good behaviour. This positive reinforcement encourages students to repeat the desired behaviors. For instance, a student who receives a sticker for good behaviour during class is likelier to behave well in the future and earn more stickers.

Negative reinforcement

Mr. Kant allows students to skip a homework assignment if they consistently participate in class discussions. Removing the homework (a negative stimulus) encourages students to engage more in discussions.

Classroom management through operant conditioning

Mrs. Dubey uses a token economy system where students earn tokens for good behaviour, such as staying on task or helping others. These tokens can later be exchanged for rewards like extra recess time or small treats. This approach leverages operant conditioning, where the reward system consistently encourages students to maintain positive behaviours.

It is important to note that while behaviourist theories provide valuable insights into learning, they only partially encompass all aspects of the learning process. Therefore, instructional designers and educators should consider other learning theories also to create effective and engaging learning experiences.

II

Cognitivist School of Thought

The Cognitivist School of Thought in education focuses on the mental processes involved in learning, emphasizing how individuals acquire, process, store, and retrieve information. Cognitivism posits that learning is an active process that interacts with prior knowledge and new information.

Educational Implications of Cognitivist Theories for Designing Instruction:

Prior Knowledge Activation

According to cognitivist theories, learners construct new knowledge based on their mental schemas or structures. As an instructional designer or trainer, you can activate learners' prior knowledge by connecting new information to what they already know. For example, before introducing a new topic, you can begin with a brief review or a pre-assessment to assess learners' existing knowledge and activate relevant concepts or experiences.

Clear Organization and Chunking of Information

Cognitivism suggests that learners have limited cognitive processing capacity, so a structured and organized presentation of information is crucial. Break down complex concepts into smaller, meaningful chunks to avoid overwhelming learners. For instance, when teaching a complicated process, divide it into logical steps and provide clear visual or textual cues to aid learners' understanding and retention.

Encourage Active Engagement and Problem-Solving

Cognitivist theories emphasize the significance of active engagement in the learning process. Instructional designers and trainers can incorporate activities and tasks requiring learners to process information actively, apply critical thinking skills, and solve problems. For example, you can design case studies, simulations, or group discussions where learners analyze real-world scenarios and propose solutions based on their cognitive abilities.

Scaffolding and Guided Practice

Cognitivism emphasizes the role of scaffolding, which involves providing temporary support to learners as they gradually master a skill or concept. As an instructional designer or trainer, you can provide guided practice, step-by-step instructions, modeling, or prompts to help learners develop their cognitive abilities. Over time, students/trainees learn to foster independent thinking and problem-solving skills without support.

Metacognitive Strategies

Cognitivist theories underscore the importance of metacognition, which refers to learners' awareness and control over their learning processes. Encourage learners to use metacognitive strategies such as setting goals, monitoring their understanding, self-evaluating, and reflecting on their learning experiences. For instance, you can incorporate activities where learners engage in self-assessment, peer feedback, or reflective journaling to promote metacognitive skills.

Multimedia and Technology Integration

Cognitivism recognizes the impact of multimedia and technology on learning. As an instructional designer, you can leverage multimedia resources such as videos, graphics, and interactive simulations to enhance learners' engagement and understanding. Additionally, consider incorporating technology-enabled learning platforms or tools that provide immediate feedback, adaptive learning experiences, and personalized instruction based on learners' cognitive abilities and progress.

The Cognitivist School of Thought suggests that instructional designers and trainers should focus on learners' cognitive processes and design instruction that promotes active engagement, prior knowledge activation, information organization, problem-solving, scaffolding, metacognitive strategies, and effective use of multimedia and technology.

These implications apply to various instructional contexts, including classroom teaching, online learning, corporate training, or any other learning environment. Using these principles, you can create compelling, engaging instructional experiences that optimize learners' cognitive abilities and promote meaningful learning outcomes.

Examples

Shared below are some examples to demonstrate how cognitivist theories can effectively create an environment conducive to learning.

Using visual aids to enhance memory

Mrs. Sharma notices that her student, Arjun, struggles to remember the steps to solve math problems. To help him, she creates a colorful chart with each step clearly outlined. Every time Arjun gets stuck, he glances at the chart, which helps him recall what to do next. Over time, the visual cues reinforce his memory, and he becomes more confident in solving problems independently.

Encouraging active learning through group discussions

Mr. Patel believes that students learn better when they actively engage with the material. In his history class, he often divides the students into small groups to discuss important events. For instance, when discussing India's independence, he asks the students, including Aisha and Rohan, to share their thoughts and connect the events to what they've learned. By talking it out, they better understand and remember the material longer.

Helping students organize information

Ms. Mehta knows that her student, Priya, has a hard time keeping track of everything she learns in science. To help, she teaches Priya to use a mind map. Together, they create a map with the main topic in the center and branches for each key idea. As Priya organizes the information visually, she finds it easier to understand and recall the concepts during tests.

These examples show how teachers like Mrs. Sharma, Mr. Patel, and Ms. Mehta use cognitivist strategies to make learning more effective and meaningful for their students.

III

Constructivist School of Thought

This chapter will explore the Constructivist School of Thought and its educational implications for designing instruction.

Constructivism is a learning theory emphasizing learners' active role in constructing knowledge through meaningful experiences. As instructional designers and trainers, understanding the principles of constructivism can help you create engaging and compelling learning experiences. Let's delve into the indispensable tenets and examples of how to apply constructivist theories in instructional design.

Learner-Centered Approach

In constructivism, the learner is at the heart of the learning process. It acknowledges that individuals come to learning situations with prior knowledge, experiences, and beliefs. Educators and facilitators should consider learners' existing mental models and design instruction that builds upon their prior knowledge. For example, when teaching a science concept such as photosynthesis, you can begin by eliciting students' existing understanding and then guide them to explore new information through hands-on activities or simulations.

Active Engagement and Social Interaction

Constructivism highlights the importance of social interaction and active engagement in learning. Learners fabricate knowledge by interacting with their environment, materials, and other learners. As instructional designers, you should design activities encouraging collaboration, discussion, and problem-solving. For instance, in a training session on leadership skills, you can organize group projects or role-playing activities that promote peer-to-peer interaction and enable learners to apply their knowledge in real-world scenarios.

Authentic and Meaningful Contexts

Constructivism emphasizes the significance of learning in authentic and meaningful contexts. Educators should strive to create learning experiences that connect to real-life situations, enabling learners to apply their knowledge practically. For example, when designing a language book, you can incorporate tasks that require learners to communicate in real-life scenarios, such as ordering food in a restaurant or participating in a simulated business negotiation.

Scaffolding and Guided Discovery

Constructivist theories advocate for providing scaffolding and guidance to support learners in their knowledge-construction process. Trainers and educators should offer support and structure, gradually fading it as learners become more proficient. This scaffolding often involves prompts, guiding questions, and a gradual release of responsibility. For instance, in teaching a complex mathematical concept, you can provide step-by-step guidance initially and gradually encourage learners to solve problems independently as their understanding deepens.

Reflection and Metacognition

Constructivism promotes reflection and metacognition, encouraging learners to think about their thinking and learning processes. As instructional designers, you can incorporate reflection activities, self-assessment tools, and opportunities for learners to articulate their understanding. For example, after completing a project, learners can reflect on their learning experience, identify challenges faced, and set goals for future improvement.

Examples

Below are some examples showing how Mrs. Fernandes, Mr. Rao, and Ms. Joshi create learning experiences that allow their students to actively build knowledge through doing, exploring, and connecting to the real world.

Learning through hands-on projects

Mrs. Fernandes loves to get her students involved in hands-on activities. When they're learning about plants, she asks them to plant seeds in small pots. Students observe the growth daily, water the plants, and take notes in their journals. By actively participating in the process, they develop a deeper understanding of how plants grow rather than just reading about it in a textbook.

Encouraging exploration and discovery

Mr. Rao likes to turn his science lessons into opportunities for discovery. When teaching about electricity, he sets up different stations with batteries, wires, and bulbs. He lets the students experiment to see how they can light the bulb. Through trial and error, students figure out how to complete the circuit independently. This exploration process helps them grasp the concept of electricity in a way that sticks with them.

Connecting lessons to real-life experiences

Ms. Joshi believes students learn best when they can relate lessons to their lives. When teaching a lesson on money, she asks her students to set up a mock store. Students use fake money to buy and sell items, learning to make changes and budget their money. By connecting the lesson to a real-world experience, they better understand the value of money and how it works in everyday life.

The Constructivist School of Thought offers valuable insights for instructional designers and trainers. Remember, instructional design should focus on facilitating knowledge construction rather than simply transmitting information.

IV
Types of Constructivism in the teaching world

In the previous chapter, we discussed the Constructivist school of thought emphasizing learners' active construction of knowledge through their experiences and interactions with the environment. It suggests that learners actively build their understanding and knowledge by connecting new information to their existing knowledge and experiences. Several types of constructivism have been developed in instructional design and training to guide educators in creating engaging learning experiences. Let's explore some of these types with suitable examples:

Cognitive Constructivism

Cognitive constructivism focuses on the mental processes involved in learning and understanding. It emphasizes the individual's active role in constructing knowledge through thinking, problem-solving, and reflection. According to this approach, learners organize new information by relating it to their prior knowledge and experiences.

Example: In a science class, students are given an open-ended problem to solve, such as designing a sustainable energy solution for their community. They construct their understanding of renewable energy sources through research, experimentation, and collaboration, considering environmental impact, efficiency, and cost-effectiveness.

Social Constructivism

Social constructivism highlights the importance of social interactions and collaboration in learning. It suggests that learners construct knowledge through dialogue, negotiation, and shared experiences with others. Learning is a social activity where learners actively participate in discussions, group projects, and cooperative learning tasks.

Example: In a history class, students create a group project to recreate a historical event. Each student takes on a role and collaborates with others to research, plan, and perform a reenactment. Through this shared experience, they construct a deeper understanding of the event, its context, and its significance.

Radical Constructivism

Radical constructivism posits that knowledge is subjective and unique to each individual. It asserts that learners construct their reality based on their experiences and interpretations. This perspective emphasizes that learning is ever-adapting and refines one's mental models.

Example: In an art class, students explore abstract painting techniques. They experiment with various materials, colors, and forms and create unique interpretations of abstract art. Through this process, they construct their understanding of aesthetics, composition, and the expressive potential of visual arts.

Psychological Constructivism

Psychological constructivism, also known as Piagetian constructivism, is based on Jean Piaget's work. It focuses on learners' cognitive development and how they construct knowledge by assimilating and accommodating new information. This approach suggests that learners actively build mental structures, called schemas, to organize and make sense of their experiences.

Example: In a mathematics class, students explore geometric shapes and their properties. They manipulate physical objects like blocks or tiles to build different patterns and observe their characteristics. Through these hands-on activities, they construct their understanding of geometric concepts, such as symmetry, angles, and transformations.

Cultural Constructivism

Cultural constructivism emphasizes the influence of cultural and societal factors on learning. It acknowledges that cultural contexts influence the construction of knowledge. This approach recognizes the diversity of learners' backgrounds, experiences, and cultural perspectives and aims to incorporate and value these differences in the learning process.

Example: In a language class, students engage in activities that expose them to various cultural practices, customs, and traditions associated with the target language. They participate in role-plays, watch videos, and engage in discussions to understand the cultural nuances embedded in the language. These activities construct a more comprehensive understanding of the language and its cultural context.

It's important to note that these types of constructivism are not mutually exclusive but act as complementary perspectives integrating with instructional design and training approaches. Meticulous instructional designers and trainers often draw on multiple types of constructivism to create meaningful and engaging learning experiences that promote active knowledge construction by the learners.

V

Introduction to Instructional Design (ID) Models

Effective instructional design facilitates meaningful learning experiences in education and training. ID models provide a systematic approach to developing instructional materials and activities, ensuring they are engaging, effective, and aligned with learning goals.

Instructional design models serve as frameworks that guide the instructional design process, offering a structured approach to analyzing, designing, developing, implementing, and evaluating instructional interventions. These models help instructional designers, educators, and trainers create cohesive and impactful learning experiences by considering learners' needs, learning objectives, content, instructional strategies, and assessment methods.

Let's explore some prominent instructional design models that have been widely adopted and proven to be effective in various educational and training settings:

ADDIE Model

The ADDIE (Analysis, Design, Development, Implementation, Evaluation) model is one of the most well-known and traditional instructional design models. It emphasizes a systematic approach, starting with analyzing learners' needs and characteristics, followed by the design, development, implementation, and evaluation stages. The ADDIE model provides a flexible, customizable framework to meet specific instructional design requirements.

SAM Model

The SAM (Successive Approximation Model) is an agile instructional design model that promotes iterative development and collaboration. It consists of three phases: preparation, iteration, and implementation. The SAM model encourages frequent feedback and evaluation, allowing instructional designers and trainers to improvise throughout the design process.

Merrill's First Principles of Instruction

This model, proposed by David Merrill, focuses on the fundamental principles of instruction. Learning experiences arise from problem-solving, activation of prior knowledge, demonstration of new skills or knowledge, application of knowledge, and integration of new knowledge into real-world contexts. Merrill's model provides a learner-centered approach that encourages active engagement and meaningful learning.

Gagne's Nine Events of Instruction

Developed by Robert Gagne, this model identifies a sequence of events that contribute to effective learning. It includes events such as gaining attention, informing learners of objectives, stimulating recall of prior knowledge, presenting new content, providing guidance for comprehending, eliciting learner performance, providing feedback, assessing performance, and enhancing knowledge retention and transfer. Gagne's model offers a structured approach to designing instructional sequences that augment learning outcomes.

Bloom's Taxonomy

Have you heard of Bloom's Taxonomy? It's a groundbreaking instructional design framework introduced by Benjamin Bloom in 1956. Since then, other educators have refined and updated it to provide a powerful tool for instructional designers. Bloom's Taxonomy is a hierarchical system, with lower-order thinking skills at the bottom and higher-order thinking skills at the top. For instructional designers, this taxonomy offers a valuable resource for creating targeted learning objectives and assessments. By carefully selecting verbs that align with each taxonomy level, designers can ensure that their objectives are measurable and specific, leading to a more focused and practical approach to cognitive skill development.

Dick and Carey Model

The Dick and Carey Model is a comprehensive instructional design approach that ensures effective content creation. This model consists of nine interconnected components that guide the instructional design process.

Action Mapping by Cathy Moore

Action Mapping is a framework developed by Cathy Moore that focuses on creating effective training solutions by identifying the specific actions learners need to take to achieve their goals. It's a practical approach that addresses the performance gap between what learners currently know or do and what they need to know or do.

These are just a few examples of the many instructional design models available. As an aspiring instructional designer or trainer, familiarizing yourself with these models and understanding their underlying principles will empower you to design and deliver engaging, effective, and learner-centered instruction.

Remember, instructional design models serve as valuable tools, but they should be adapted and customized to suit your learners' unique needs and contexts. As you embark on your journey to becoming an instructional designer or trainer, keep exploring, learning, and refining your instructional design skills to create impactful learning experiences for your future learners.

VI
Characteristics of different ID Models

In the previous chapter, we discussed how several ID models can guide your approach to creating practical learning experiences. These models provide systematic frameworks for analyzing, developing, implementing, and evaluating instructional materials and methods. This chapter will focus on some of the critical characteristics of different instructional design models, along with suitable examples:

ADDIE Model (Analysis, Design, Development, Implementation, Evaluation)

The ADDIE model is one of the most widely used instructional design models. It consists of five sequential phases that guide the development of instructional materials.

- *Analysis:* In this phase, you gather information about the learners, their needs, and the learning context. For example, you might conduct interviews, surveys, or needs assessments to identify the learning objectives.
- *Design:* Here, you define the learning objectives, select appropriate instructional strategies, and determine the content and assessment methods. You may create storyboards or prototypes to outline the structure and flow of the instruction.

- ***Development:*** This phase involves creating the instructional materials based on the design specifications. It includes writing content, developing multimedia elements, and creating assessments.
- ***Implementation:*** The developed instruction is delivered to the learners. This phase involves managing the learning environment, training instructors, and conducting formative evaluations.
- ***Evaluation:*** The effectiveness of the instruction is assessed through various means, such as tests, surveys, or observations. Feedback is collected and used to improve future iterations of the pedagogy.

Example: Suppose you are designing an online book on graphic design. You would start by analyzing the learners' needs, blueprinting the book structure, developing the instructional materials (videos, quizzes, etc.), implementing the book on a learning management system, and evaluating the learners' performance and book effectiveness.

SAM Model (Successive Approximation Model)

The SAM model emphasizes an iterative and agile approach to instructional design. It consists of three phases in cyclic repetition: Preparation, Iterative Design, and Evaluation.

- ***Preparation:*** In this phase, you gather information, identify goals, and plan the project. You establish the design and development team, define the project scope, and set expectations.
- ***Iterative Design:*** This phase involves rapid prototyping and review cycles. You create a rough prototype of the instructional materials, receive feedback from stakeholders, make necessary revisions, and refine the design.
- ***Evaluation:*** The prototype is evaluated against the defined goals and objectives. Feedback is gathered from users, and the results are used to inform subsequent iterations. The process continues until the desired level of quality and effectiveness is achieved.

Example: Imagine you are designing a sales training program for a company. You would start by preparing the project, defining the learning goals and target audience. Then, you would create a prototype of the training materials, seek feedback from sales representatives, make improvements based on their input, and repeat this cycle until the program meets the desired outcomes.

Merrill's First Principles of Instruction

Merrill's model focuses on five core principles that guide instructional design. These principles are:

- **Activation:** Engage learners by stimulating their existing knowledge and experiences.
- **Demonstration:** Present clear examples and demonstrations of the desired performance.
- **Application:** Provide space and opportunity for learners to apply their knowledge and practice skills.
- **Integration:** Motivate learners to relate new knowledge to existing knowledge.
- **Reflection:** Encourage learners to reflect on their learning and receive feedback.

Example: Suppose you are designing a training program for new software users. You would activate learners' prior knowledge by asking them about their experience with similar software, demonstrating the software's features through interactive tutorials, providing hands-on exercises for learners to practice using the software, encouraging them to relate new functions to their previous knowledge, and finally, provide time for reflection and feedback on their progress.

Gagne's Nine Events of Instruction

In 1965, Robert Gagné devised a brilliant idea - a series of events that could pave the way for effective learning. These events were about getting the students' minds in the right place and making learning engaging and meaningful. And let me tell you, and they're still just as relevant today.

So let's dive into Gagné's nine events of instruction.

First, we've got **"Gain the attention of the students."** It's all about capturing their focus and getting them ready to learn. How? You could surprise them with something new and exciting or get their brains buzzing with thought-provoking questions. You could even have them break the ice with an activity. The key is to spark their curiosity.

Next on the list is *"Inform students of the objectives."* Students need to know what they're aiming for, right? So tell them! Let them in on the goals of the course and each lesson. It'll give them a clear understanding of what they're meant to learn and do. And remember to include those objectives right from the start.

Moving on to *"Stimulate recall of prior learning."* Help students connect new information to things they already know. Ask them about their experiences or relate new concepts to what they've learned. It's all about making those connections and building on their existing knowledge.

Now it's time to *"Present the content."* This is where you show students the good stuff. Use different strategies to present the lesson content - videos, demos, lectures; you name it. And remember to organize the information in a way that makes sense. Oh, and explain things after showing them how it's done.

Next up is *"Provide learning guidance."* Give students some tips and tricks to help them along the way. Show them the resources available and guide them on how to make the most of them. Because let's face it, learning how to learn is a skill.

Now comes the moment of truth - *"Elicit performance."* Time for the students to put what they've learned into action. It's all about applying their newfound skills and knowledge. Get them involved in activities, have them work together, and give them opportunities to show what they can do.

Then we've got *"Reinforce performance."* This is where you give students feedback and help them improve. It's all about assessing their understanding and keeping them on the right track.

Give students feedback on time to make sure they're on track and to help them improve. This way, they can recognize areas to improve before it's too late. Here are some different types of feedback you can give to students:

- Confirmatory feedback: Let them know they did what they were supposed to do. It doesn't point out specific areas for improvement but encourages them to continue.
- Evaluative feedback: Tell them how accurate their performance was, but wait to guide them on what to do next.
- Remedial feedback: Direct them to find the correct answer without giving it away.

- Descriptive or analytic feedback: Offer suggestions, directions, and information to help them improve.
- Peer evaluation and self-evaluation can also help students identify where they need to improve their and their peers' work.

Event 8 is **"Assess Progress"** - Check if students have achieved the learning outcomes in the course objectives.

Here are some methods for testing learning:

- Use pre-and post-tests to measure how students have progressed in understanding the content or skills.
- Incorporate formative assessments throughout instruction, like asking questions, engaging in active learning activities, or giving quizzes.
- Use various assessment methods so students have multiple opportunities to show their proficiency.
- Develop clear and effective rubrics to assess written assignments, projects, or presentations.

And last but not least- **"Make Learning Stick"** - help students retain information by connecting course concepts to real-world applications.

Here are some methods to help students internalize new knowledge:

- Connect course concepts with prior and future concepts to reinforce connections and build on what they already know.
- Include questions from previous tests in future exams to reinforce the course material.
- Have students convert information into different formats, like creating a concept map to show connections between ideas.
- Clearly state your lesson goals and use them to guide your instructional design. Align learning activities with those goals to promote deep learning.

Bloom's Taxonomy

Let's delve into the levels of Bloom's Taxonomy:

- **Knowledge:** Tap into prior knowledge by retrieving essential facts, definitions, and concepts from long-term memory.
- **Comprehension:** Dive deeper into understanding by using effective strategies and interpreting, summarizing, and explaining information.
- **Application:** Take knowledge to the next level by applying it in practical situations, solving problems, and transferring concepts to new contexts.
- **Analyzing:** Break complex information into smaller parts, identifying patterns, relationships, and cause-and-effect connections. Ensure that these parts are relevant to each other and the overall goal.
- **Evaluating:** Critique and assess information based on predefined learning criteria. Develop a critical eye for quality and relevance.
- **Creating:** Bring it all together by organizing ideas into a new structure, forming a coherent understanding pattern, and unleashing your creativity and innovation.

Example: Suppose you are training a group on customer service skills. At level 1, learners would recall fundamental concepts, definitions, and key principles. Activities at this level could include memorization of key terms, definitions, and simple customer interaction scenarios. Level 2 can be achieved by asking the learners to summarize customer service principles and discussing different types of customer expectations. Role-playing exercises, case studies, and simulations can be effective activities to apply customer service skills. You can then ask learners to analyze different customer scenarios, identify underlying issues, and assess the effectiveness of different communication approaches. Levels 5 and 6 can be achieved by assessing the appropriateness of learners' responses and making recommendations for improvement and giving learners projects that involve creating customer service manuals, designing training workshops, or proposing improvements to existing customer service processes.

Dick and Carey Model

The nine components of Dick and Carey model are discussed below:

- **Set clear goals:** Clearly define the specific learning goals and objectives the instruction aims to achieve.
- **Conduct thorough analysis:**Analyze the instructional content and identify the specific skills and knowledge learners need to acquire to

meet the set goals.

- ***Understand learners and context:*** Consider the learners' characteristics and the context of content delivery, including their prior knowledge, skills, and the learning environment.
- ***Define performance objectives:*** Set performance objectives clearly describing what learners should be able to do after completing the training program.
- ***Develop assessments:*** Create assessments that measure learners' progress and determine if they have achieved the objectives.
- ***Create a strategy:*** Develop a detailed instructional plan outlining the specific methods and materials to deliver the instruction.
- ***Select instructional materials:*** Choose the appropriate instructional materials and media, such as textbooks, videos, and interactive multimedia, to effectively deliver the instruction.
- ***Conduct formative evaluation:*** Test the effectiveness of the instruction through formative assessment and identify areas for improvement.
- ***Revise and improve:*** Use the feedback and results from the formative evaluation to revise and enhance the instruction.

Example: You can use the Dick and Carey ID model to effectively enhance leadership and delegation skills among employees. In this context, the model's systematic approach can be applied as follows:

- Analysis: Identify the target audience's current leadership and delegation competencies. Assess their needs, knowledge gaps, and performance goals.
- Design: Develop clear learning objectives such as understanding leadership styles, communication, and decision-making. Create engaging content through case studies, role-playing, and interactive scenarios, emphasizing the importance of effective delegation.
- Development: Craft comprehensive training materials, including e-learning modules and hands-on activities. Incorporate real-life examples that mirror workplace situations to enhance relevancy.
- Implementation: Deliver the training using a blend of online resources and in-person workshops. Encourage active participation and group discussions to reinforce learning.
- Evaluation: Employ pre- and post-assessments to measure skill improvements. Gather feedback from participants to refine the program.

- Revision: Based on assessment results and feedback, refine the content and activities to make the training even more effective.

Action Mapping by Cathy Moore

Critical Steps of Action Mapping are:

- *Identify the Goal:* Start by clarifying the desired performance outcome. What should learners be able to do by the end of the training?
- *Identify the Action:* Break down the goal into specific actions that learners must perform to achieve the desired outcome. These actions should be observable and measurable.
- *Identify the Barriers:* Determine the obstacles or challenges that prevent learners from taking the desired actions, including a need for more knowledge, skills, resources, or motivation.
- *Identify the Knowledge and Skills:* Identify the specific knowledge and skills required to overcome the barriers and successfully perform the desired actions.
- *Design Learning Activities:* Develop learning activities that address the KSA (knowledge, skills, and attitude) needed to overcome the barriers. These activities should be engaging and realistic, simulating the context in which learners will apply their skills.
- *Engage and Motivate:* Integrate elements that motivate and engage learners. Show them the real-world relevance of their learning and how it connects to their goals.
- *Evaluate and Refine:* Continuously assess the effectiveness of the training by measuring whether learners can perform the desired actions. Based on feedback, refine the training to improve outcomes.

Example: Let's apply Action Mapping to a customer service training scenario.

- Identify the Goal: Improve customer service representatives' ability to handle customer complaints effectively.
- Identify the Action: Break down the goal into specific actions:

  ◦ Listen actively to the customer's complaint.

- Empathize with the customer's frustration.
- Offer a solution or escalate the issue as needed.
- Ensure the customer is satisfied before ending the interaction.

- Identify the Barriers: Potential barriers could include:

  - Lack of active listening skills.
  - Inability to empathize due to a scripted approach.
  - Need for knowledge about company policies and products.

- Identify the Knowledge and Skills: Training should cover:

  - Active listening techniques.
  - Empathy-building exercises.
  - In-depth understanding of company policies and products.

- Design Learning Activities:

  - Scenario-based simulations where learners practice handling various customer complaints.
  - Role-playing exercises that focus on demonstrating empathy.
  - Interactive modules that provide detailed information on company policies and products.

- Engage and Motivate:

  - Showcase real customer stories to highlight the impact of effective complaint handling.
  - Emphasize the value of satisfied customers to the company's success.

- Evaluate and Refine:

  - Use role-playing assessments to gauge learners' skill development.
  - Gather feedback from both learners and supervisors about the effectiveness of the training.
  - Adjust the training based on feedback to enhance its impact.

So, there you have it.

These are just a few examples of instructional design models, each with its characteristics and suitability for different contexts. As an instructional designer or trainer, it's essential to familiarize yourself with these models and adapt them to meet the specific needs of your learners and learning objectives. Remember, effective instructional design requires a systematic and learner-centered approach.

VII

Educational Implications of ID Models

So far, we've seen that instructional design models focus on learner-centered approaches and emphasize active engagement, collaboration, and the construction of knowledge.

Now, let's explore each model.

The 5E Model

The 5E model is a widely used Constructivist ID model. It comprises five phases: Engage, Explore, Explain, Elaborate, and Evaluate. Each stage has a specific purpose and guides the instructional design process.

- Engage: The Engage phase aims to capture learners' attention and activate their prior knowledge to connect with new concepts. For example, a science teacher could use a video or real-world examples to introduce a new scientific concept.
- Explore: In the Explore phase, learners actively investigate and explore the topic through hands-on activities, experiments, or problem-solving tasks. This exploration encourages them to construct their understanding. For instance, students could conduct experiments to understand the laws of motion in a physics class.

- Explain: The Explain phase provides learners with explanations, information, and concepts related to the topic. Teachers or instructional materials clarify misconceptions, present new information, and demonstrate key concepts. This phase supports learners in building a solid foundation of knowledge.
- Elaborate: In the Elaborate phase; learners apply their understanding to real-life situations, connect with other concepts, and extend their learning. This phase could involve group projects, discussions, or case studies. For example, students might collaborate to design and build a model that demonstrates the principles of sustainable architecture.
- Evaluate: The Evaluate phase assesses learners' understanding and mastery of the topic. It includes formative and summative assessments such as quizzes, projects, or presentations. Evaluation provides feedback to learners and instructors, helping to improve future instruction.

Problem-Based Learning (PBL)

Problem-Based Learning is another Constructivist ID model that promotes active learning through real-world problem-solving. In PBL, learners work collaboratively in small groups to solve complex, authentic problems. Here's how PBL typically works:

- Identify a problem or scenario related to the learning objectives.
- Engage learners in the problem by presenting an authentic, challenging situation.
- Encourage learners to brainstorm and generate hypotheses, questions, and potential solutions.
- Facilitate learners' independent research to gather information and resources.
- Guide learners in analyzing the information, identifying relevant concepts, and developing strategies to solve the problem.
- Allow learners to present their findings, solutions, and reflections.

Participatory Design Model

The Participatory Design Model involves learners actively participating in designing and developing instructional materials. This collaborative approach promotes learner engagement and empowers learners to take ownership of their learning experience. For example, in a corporate training setting, learners could be involved in designing an e-learning module by contributing their ideas, suggesting relevant content, and providing feedback on the learning materials.

Anchored Instruction

Anchored Instruction is a model that uses realistic, complex problems or scenarios as the focal point for learning. These "anchors" provide a meaningful context for learners to explore and develop their understanding of concepts and skills. For instance, in a science class, students might investigate a simulated ecological problem, such as the impact of pollution on a local ecosystem. This problem-solving activity allows Students to apply scientific principles and better understand the topic.

Cognitive Apprenticeship

The Cognitive Apprenticeship model draws upon the traditional apprenticeship approach and focuses on the transfer of expertise from an experienced practitioner (the "expert") to a less experienced learner (the "apprentice"). This model emphasizes authentic tasks, coaching, and mentoring. For example, in a healthcare training program, medical students could learn by observing and working alongside experienced doctors, gradually taking on more responsibility and engaging in reflective discussions to deepen their understanding of medical practice.

Generative Learning

Generative Learning encourages learners to actively construct their knowledge by connecting new information with their existing understanding. Learners engage in meaningful activities, such as problem-solving, reflection, and concept mapping, to build mental models and make sense of new concepts. In a mathematics classroom, students may be given a challenging problem to solve collaboratively. Through this process, they generate multiple strategies, discuss their reasoning, and construct a deeper understanding of mathematical concepts and problem-solving techniques.

Discovery Learning

Discovery Learning promotes active exploration and inquiry, allowing learners to discover and construct knowledge through firsthand experiences. Learners are encouraged to explore, experiment, and draw conclusions based on their observations. For instance, in a biology class, students might investigate the process of photosynthesis by conducting experiments, making observations, and analyzing their findings. This hands-on approach fosters critical thinking, problem-solving skills, and a deeper understanding of scientific concepts.

Computer-Supported Intentional Learning Environments (CSILE)

CSILE uses computer-based tools and technologies to support collaborative learning and knowledge construction. These environments allow learners to engage in online discussions, share ideas, and build knowledge. For example, an online discussion forum can be used in a language learning book, where students share their thoughts on a specific topic, exchange feedback, and collectively construct a deeper understanding of the language and culture.

Interpretation Construction Design Model

The Interpretation Construction Design Model emphasizes the role of learners as active meaning-makers. It focuses on interpreting and constructing meaning from multiple perspectives, often using authentic, real-world problems. For instance, in a social studies class, students could engage in a project-based learning activity to analyze historical events from different perspectives, critically evaluate primary sources, and construct their interpretations of the past.

Mind Tools

Mind Tools are cognitive tools, such as software applications, simulations, or concept mapping tools, that support learners in thinking, problem-solving, and knowledge construction. These tools provide scaffolding and assistance to learners, enabling them to engage in complex tasks and develop higher-order thinking skills. Concept mapping software is an example of a mind tool that helps learners visually organize and connect ideas, facilitating more profound understanding and knowledge construction.

Remember, instructional designers and trainers can combine elements from these constructivist ID models based on the learners' learning goals, context, and needs. By applying these models, instructional designers can create engaging and effective learning experiences that promote active participation, collaboration, and knowledge construction.

Educational Implications of Instructional Design Models

Different instructional design models have unique educational implications. Here are a few inferences of various ID models for instructional designers and trainers:

Behaviourist ID Models: Behaviourist models, such as the ADDIE model (Analysis, Design, Development, Implementation, Evaluation), focus on clear objectives, step-by-step instructional sequencing, and measurable outcomes. Implications include:

- Defining clear learning objectives and aligning them with instructional activities and assessments.
- Designing structured learning materials with a focus on repetition and reinforcement.
- Developing assessments that measure specific learning outcomes and provide feedback for improvement.

Cognitivist ID Models: Cognitivist models, like Gagne's Nine Events of Instruction, emphasize the mental processes of learning, including attention, memory, and problem-solving. Implications include:

- Designing instruction that engages learners' attention, activates prior knowledge, and facilitates information processing.
- Sequencing instruction logically starts with simple concepts and gradually progresses to more complex ones.

- Incorporating strategies like chunking, scaffolding, and mnemonics to enhance learners' memory and understanding.

Constructivist ID Models: Constructivist models, as discussed earlier, prioritize learner-centered approaches, collaboration, and active learning. Implications include:

- Designing learning experiences that encourage exploration, discovery, and problem-solving.
- Incorporating opportunities for learners to engage in hands-on activities, experiments, and real-world applications.
- Facilitating collaborative learning environments where learners can interact, discuss, and construct knowledge.

Connectivist ID Models: Connectivist models, such as Siemens' Connectivism, focus on using technology, networks, and social learning. Implications include:

- Designing instruction that leverages digital tools, online resources, and social media platforms.
- Encouraging learners to connect with experts, peers, and communities of practice to extend their learning.
- Incorporating opportunities for learners to evaluate and curate information from diverse sources critically.

It's important to note that these models are not mutually exclusive, and instructional designers often integrate elements from multiple models based on the learning context and objectives.

VIII

Learner's Characteristics - Learning Styles

As educators, it's essential to understand learners' characteristics and different learning styles to design effective instructional materials and training programs. By recognizing and catering to learners' diverse needs and preferences, instructional designers and trainers can create engaging and impactful learning experiences. Let's explore learner characteristics, various learning styles, and suitable examples.

Learner's Characteristics

Learners possess unique traits and attributes influencing their learning process. Understanding these characteristics helps instructional designers tailor instruction to meet learners' needs. Some common learner characteristics include:

- *Prior Knowledge:* Learners enter educational settings with varying levels of existing knowledge and experiences. Their prior knowledge can impact how they interpret and comprehend new information. For instance, if you're designing a training program on project management, some learners may have prior experience, while others may be entirely new to the subject. Considering this diversity, the instructional material should cater to novice and experienced learners.

- ***Motivation:*** Learners' motivation levels significantly impact their engagement and learning outcomes. Motivation can be intrinsic (driven by personal interests and curiosity) or extrinsic (influenced by external factors like rewards or recognition). Instructional designers can leverage this characteristic to enhance learners' motivation by incorporating interactive activities, gamification elements, or real-life scenarios.
- ***Learning Preferences:*** Learners have different preferences when acquiring knowledge. Some may prefer visual aids, while others may prefer auditory or hands-on activities. Identifying and accommodating these preferences can enhance learners' comprehension and retention. For instance, visual learners in a software training program may benefit from graphical representations and diagrams, while kinesthetic learners may prefer interactive simulations.
- ***Learning Pace:*** Individuals learn at different speeds, and their pace can vary based on the complexity of the subject matter. Some learners may grasp concepts quickly, while others require more time and practice. Providing flexible learning options, such as self-paced modules or additional resources for further study, can cater to learners with different pace preferences.

Learning Styles

Learning styles refer to how individuals process and assimilate information. Understanding these styles can help instructional designers present content in a manner that resonates with learners. Although the concept of learning styles is debated among researchers, it's still helpful to consider different modalities through which learners engage with information. Some commonly recognized learning styles are:

- ***Visual Learners:*** Visual learners comprehend information better through visual aids - videos, images, diagrams, and charts. They benefit from visual representations that facilitate concept understanding. For example, in a biology class, visual learners may better grasp a cell's structure by studying a labeled diagram.
- ***Auditory Learners:*** Auditory learners grasp information verbally and prefer learning through listening. They benefit from lectures,

discussions, and audio resources. For instance, in a language learning program, auditory learners may benefit from listening to native speakers or participating in conversational activities.

- ***Kinesthetic Learners:*** Kinesthetic learners learn through physical activities and hands-on experiences. They thrive in environments that allow them to engage in practical tasks and manipulate objects. For example, in a science class, kinesthetic learners may better understand the concept of gravity by conducting experiments and observing its effects.

- ***Reading/Writing Learners:*** Reading/writing learners prefer text-based materials, including textbooks, articles, and written assignments. They engage best when they can read and write about the subject matter. Reading/writing learners may prefer analyzing and writing essays about literary works in a literature book.

It's important to note that learners often exhibit a combination of learning styles, and it's beneficial to incorporate multiple modalities into the instructional design to cater to different preferences.

To create effective instructional materials and training programs, instructional designers and trainers should consider these learner characteristics and learning styles and adapt content and activities accordingly. By doing so, they can engage learners, improve comprehension, and promote successful learning outcomes.

IX

Designing Learning - Design Learning Resources

Learning resources are vital in engaging learners, promoting knowledge acquisition, and enhancing the learning experience. In this chapter, we will delve into the process of designing learning resources and provide suitable examples for aspiring instructional designers and trainers.

Analyze the Learning Objectives

Before designing learning resources, it is crucial to clearly understand the learning objectives. Learning objectives define what learners should be able to do or know after completing the learning experience. Analyzing learning objectives helps instructional designers align the content and activities with the desired outcomes. For example, if the learning objective is to develop problem-solving skills, the learning resources should incorporate relevant scenarios, case studies, or interactive activities that encourage critical thinking.

Choose Appropriate Formats

Once the learning objectives are established, selecting appropriate formats for the learning resources is essential. Different formats cater to various learning styles and preferences, enhancing learner engagement and knowledge retention. Some standard formats include:

- Text-based Resources: These include instructional manuals, textbooks, handouts, and articles. They are suitable for conveying theoretical concepts, definitions, and explanations.
- Multimedia Resources: These encompass videos, audio recordings, podcasts, and interactive presentations. Multimedia resources can effectively convey complex information, demonstrate procedures, showcase real-world examples, and engage learners through visual and auditory stimuli.
- Interactive Resources: These resources actively involve learners in the learning process. Examples include simulations, games, quizzes, online discussions, and virtual reality experiences. Interactive resources foster learner engagement, promote active learning, and provide opportunities for practice and feedback.

Create Engaging Content

Engaging content is crucial for capturing learners' attention and maintaining their interest throughout the learning experience. Here are some strategies to create engaging learning resources:

- Visual Design: Use visually appealing layouts, images, and graphics to enhance the aesthetics of the learning resources. A clear and organized content layout improves readability and comprehension.
- Storytelling: Incorporate narratives or scenarios to contextualize the learning content. Story-based resources can captivate learners, facilitate information retention, and promote emotional connection.
- Interactivity: Embed interactive elements, such as clickable buttons, drag-and-drop activities, or branching scenarios, to encourage learner participation. The interactivity boosts engagement and provides opportunities for immediate feedback.

Ensure Accessibility and Inclusivity

Designing learning resources accessible to diverse learners is essential for inclusive education. Consider the following aspects:

- Text Accessibility: Use readable fonts, appropriate font sizes, and sufficient color contrast for easy reading. Give alternative text for images and ensure proper heading structure.
- Multimedia Accessibility: Provide closed captions, video transcripts, and audio descriptions for visuals and ensure compatibility with assistive technologies.
- Universal Design: Implement universal design principles to accommodate learners with different abilities and learning preferences. Offer multiple formats or options for accessing the content.

Designing potent learning resources requires careful consideration of learning objectives, appropriate formats, engaging content, and accessibility. By aligning resources with learning objectives, employing diverse structures, creating captivating content, and ensuring accessibility, instructional designers and trainers can enhance the overall learning experience for their audience. Remember, the ultimate goal is to empower learners and facilitate their journey toward acquiring new knowledge and skills.

X

Evaluation of Learning - Models of Evaluation

An essential component of an instructional designer's/trainer's work is evaluating learning outcomes. Evaluation of learning refers to assessing and measuring the effectiveness of instructional methods, materials, and strategies used in a learning environment. It helps educators determine whether the desired learning outcomes are being achieved and provides insights into how to improve the instructional process. In this chapter, we will explore the evaluation of learning, its importance, and various models and approaches that instructional designers and trainers can employ.

Understanding Evaluation of Learning

Evaluation of learning involves systematically gathering and analyzing data to determine the effectiveness of instructional programs and materials. It helps identify strengths, weaknesses, and areas for improvement, allowing designers and trainers to make informed decisions to enhance the learning experience. Here are the key elements of the evaluation of learning:

- *Purpose:* The evaluation should align with the overall goals and objectives of the instructional program or training initiative.
- *Criteria:* Clearly defined criteria are essential to assess the scale to which learning objectives have been achieved. These criteria include knowledge acquisition, skills development, attitude change, and overall learner

satisfaction.

- ***Data Collection:*** Evaluation data can be gathered through various methods, such as tests, observations, surveys, interviews, and focus groups. The collected data should be relevant, reliable, and valid.
- ***Analysis:*** The collected data is then analyzed to draw meaningful insights and conclusions about the effectiveness of the learning experience. Statistical, qualitative, and comparative analyses can be used for this purpose.
- ***Feedback and Improvement:*** Based on the analysis, feedback is provided to stakeholders, including trainers, learners, and program sponsors. This feedback helps identify areas for improvement and informs future instructional design decisions.

Models of Evaluation

Several evaluation models offer a systematic framework for assessing learning outcomes. Here, we will explore some widely used evaluation models:

Kirkpatrick's Four Levels of Evaluation

Donald Kirkpatrick's model provides a hierarchical approach to evaluation. It consists of four levels:

Level 1: Reaction - Measures learners' initial response to the learning experience through surveys or feedback forms.

Level 2: Learning - Assesses learners' knowledge acquisition, skills, and attitudes through multiple tests and assessments.

Level 3: Behaviour - Evaluate the transfer of learning into practical application in the workplace or real-life scenarios.

Level 4: Results - Measures the impact of the learning program on organizational goals and outcomes.

Phillips' ROI Model

The Return on Investment (ROI) model, developed by Jack Phillips, evaluates the monetary benefits of a training program. It involves assessing the costs incurred, both direct and indirect and comparing them with the financial gains resulting from the training initiative.

Let's understand this better with the help of an example.

Ms. Kapoor is the HR manager at TechWave, a mid-sized company. She recently organized a customer service training program for the support team, including employees like Priya and Amit. The training aimed to improve customer satisfaction and reduce response times.

Step 1: Reaction

After the training, Ms. Kapoor gathered feedback from Priya and Amit to see how they felt about the training. They both found the content engaging and relevant. Priya mentioned that she appreciated the practical examples, while Amit said the role-playing exercises helped him understand how to handle difficult customers.

Step 2: Learning

Next, Ms. Kapoor evaluates what Priya and Amit actually learned. She gives them a short quiz on customer service techniques they covered in the training. Priya and Amit scored well, showing they've grasped the key concepts.

Step 3: Application

A few weeks after the training, Ms. Kapoor observed how Priya and Amit applied their knowledge. She noticed that Priya now uses a more structured approach when handling customer queries, and Amit is more confident in resolving issues on the first call, indicating that they were applying the skills from the training to their daily work.

Step 4: Business Impact

Ms. Kapoor measures the impact by comparing customer satisfaction scores and response times before and after the training. She sees a 15% improvement in customer satisfaction and a 20% reduction in response times, indicating that the training has positively impacted the business.

Step 5: ROI Calculation

Finally, Ms. Kapoor calculates the training's ROI. She considers the costs of the training program, including materials and the time Priya and Amit spent in training, which total $5,000. Improving customer satisfaction and efficiency is estimated to bring in an additional $15,000 in revenue over the next year. Using Phillips' ROI formula, she calculates an ROI of 200% ($15,000 in benefits minus $5,000 in costs, divided by $5,000).

Ms. Kapoor concludes that the customer service training program was successful and provided TechWave with a strong return on investment.

The Success Case Method

The Success Case Method, proposed by Robert Brinkerhoff, identifies and examines successful and unsuccessful cases of learning outcomes. It involves selecting a small sample of learners who achieved exceptional results or faced challenges. This enables trainers to gain valuable insights to improve learners' learning experience by analyzing the reasons behind their success or failure.

Let's look at an example to understand the method better.

Mr. Iyer is the training manager at a retail company called FashionLine. He recently organized a sales training program for store managers, including employees such as Ananya and Ravi. The training was designed to help them improve their sales techniques and increase store revenue.

Step 1: Identifying the Best and Worst Cases

A few months after the training, Mr. Iyer evaluates its effectiveness using the Success Case Method. He starts by identifying the best and worst cases—those with the most and least success with the training. Through performance data and feedback, he finds that Ananya has significantly increased her store's sales, while Ravi's sales numbers haven't changed much.

Step 2: Investigating the Best Cases

Mr. Iyer interviewed Ananya to understand what worked for her. Ananya explains that the training was beneficial, particularly the role-playing exercises that taught her how to better connect with customers. She's been using these techniques consistently, and as a result, her store's sales have gone up by 25%. Ananya also mentioned that the training gave her new confidence in leading her team.

Step 3: Investigating the Least Successful Cases

Mr. Iyer then speaks with Ravi to understand why the training didn't have the same impact on him. While he enjoyed the training, Ravi admits he struggled to apply the techniques in his day-to-day work. He found it challenging to change his usual approach, so his sales numbers stayed the same. Ravi also shared that he felt he needed more follow-up support after the training to help him implement the new strategies.

Step 4: Analyzing the Findings

With these insights, Mr. Iyer compares Ananya's and Ravi's experiences. He realizes that the training was effective for those who fully embraced the new techniques and had the confidence to apply them, like Ananya.

However, it wasn't as effective for those who needed additional support, like Ravi.

Step 5: Making Improvements

Based on these findings, Mr. Iyer improved the training program by adding follow-up coaching sessions to help employees like Ravi better apply what they've learned. He also considers creating more personalized support to address individual challenges.

Through the Success Case Method, Mr. Iyer can see what worked well in the training and what needs improvement, allowing him to make the program more effective for everyone at FashionLine.

Kaufman's Model of Learning Evaluation

Kaufman's Model, developed by Dr. Roger Kaufman, focuses on evaluating learning outcomes based on five levels of evaluation. It emphasizes the importance of aligning learning goals with organizational goals and measuring the impact of learning interventions. The five levels of evaluation are:

Level 1: Input Evaluation - This level examines the quality and adequacy of the resources and materials used in the learning program. It assesses factors like the relevance of content, instructional methods, and instructional materials. For example, an input evaluation for a sales training program would consider whether the topic covers essential selling skills and if the instructional materials, such as case studies and simulations, are effective.

Level 2: Process Evaluation - This level focuses on evaluating the actual implementation of the learning program. It assesses how well the program was delivered, including factors like instructional design, teaching methods, and learner engagement. For instance, a process evaluation for a leadership development workshop would analyze whether the facilitator used interactive activities, encouraged discussions, and effectively engaged participants.

Level 3: Outcome Evaluation - This level measures the immediate impact of the learning program on learners. It assesses whether the desired learning outcomes, such as knowledge acquisition, skill development, or attitude change, were achieved. For example, an outcome evaluation for a software training program would involve assessing whether the participants acquired the necessary skills to use the software effectively.

Level 4: Impact Evaluation - This level examines the broader impact of the learning program on the organization and its stakeholders. It assesses the extent to which the learning outcomes have translated into tangible improvements in performance, productivity, or organizational goals. For instance, an impact evaluation for a customer service training program would analyze whether the training resulted in increased customer satisfaction ratings or reduced complaint rates.

Level 5: Return on Investment (ROI) Evaluation - This level determines the financial return or value gained from the learning program. It assesses the program's cost-effectiveness by comparing its benefits and costs. ROI evaluation could involve calculating the monetary value of increased sales revenue due to a sales training program compared to the program's cost.

Anderson's Value of Learning Model

Anderson's Value of Learning Model, developed by Dr. Genevieve Brown Anderson, focuses on measuring the value of learning from both an individual and organizational perspective. It emphasizes the importance of aligning learning outcomes with strategic goals and determining the return on learning investment. The model comprises four dimensions:

Dimension 1 - Individual Value: This dimension evaluates the impact of learning on individual learners. It considers improved job performance, increased job satisfaction, career advancement opportunities, and personal growth. For example, a marketing training program that helps individuals acquire new digital marketing skills can enhance their value in the job market and increase their chances of career progression.

Dimension 2 - Organizational Value: This dimension examines how learning contributes to organizational success. It assesses factors like increased productivity, improved customer satisfaction, enhanced innovation, and reduced turnover. For instance, a cybersecurity training program that enhances employees' knowledge and skills in data protection can help an organization mitigate risks, prevent data breaches, and maintain its reputation.

Dimension 3 - Stakeholder Value: This dimension focuses on the impact of learning on external stakeholders, such as customers, clients, or the community. It considers improved products or services, better customer experiences, and positive social impact. For example, a training program for healthcare professionals that enhances patient care practices can improve health outcomes and increase patient satisfaction.

Dimension 4 - Strategic Value: This dimension evaluates the alignment between learning outcomes and strategic organizational goals. It assesses whether the learning program contributes to long-term corporate strategies, such as entering new markets, developing new products, or improving operational efficiency. For instance, a leadership development program that nurtures future leaders aligns with an organization's strategic goal of building a capable leadership pipeline.

Using Anderson's Value of Learning Model, instructional designers and trainers can showcase their learning programs' broader value and impact beyond immediate outcomes, helping organizations make informed decisions about investing in learning initiatives.

These models provide valuable frameworks for instructional designers and trainers to evaluate the effectiveness of their programs and demonstrate the value they bring to learners and organizations. By utilizing these models, aspiring instructional designers and trainers can design, implement, and evaluate learning experiences that align with organizational goals and deliver measurable results.

Types of Evaluation

Formative Evaluation

Formative evaluation occurs during instructional design and development. Its purpose is to gather feedback and make improvements before the final implementation. It involves ongoing assessments, observations, and feedback mechanisms to track student progress and ascertain areas that require adjustment. Formative evaluation provides valuable insights for instructional designers and trainers to refine their materials and methods.

Summative Evaluation

Summative evaluation occurs at the end of a learning module, book, or program. It focuses on measuring the overall achievement of learning outcomes. Summative evaluation methods include tests, quizzes, projects, portfolios, and other assessments that determine the level of students' desired knowledge and skills. The results of summative evaluations help trainers and instructional designers ascertain the effectiveness of their instructional strategies.

Diagnostic Evaluation

Diagnostic evaluation aims to identify learners' strengths and weaknesses before instruction begins. It helps trainers and instructional designers gain insights into learners' prior knowledge, skills, and misconceptions, allowing them to tailor their instructional approach. Diagnostic evaluation methods may include pre-tests, interviews, surveys, or self-assessment activities.

Norm-Referenced Evaluation

The norm-referenced evaluation compares an individual's performance against the performance of a group or a predefined standard. It determines how learners in a group rank in comparison. Commonly used norm-referenced evaluations include standardized tests like SAT, GRE, or IQ tests. Norm-referenced evaluations provide information about learners' strengths and weaknesses in a broader context.

Criterion-Referenced Evaluation

Criterion-referenced evaluation measures learners' performance against specific criteria or predetermined standards. The focus is determining whether learners have achieved specific learning objectives or competency levels. Powerful tools like rubrics, checklists, and performance-based assessments enhance the evaluation process. This type of evaluation helps trainers and instructional designers assess the mastery of specific skills and knowledge.

Self-Evaluation

Self-evaluation encourages learners to reflect on their learning progress and assess their strengths and weaknesses. It promotes self-awareness, metacognition, and self-directed learning. Self-evaluation methods include self-assessment quizzes, journals, portfolios, or peer feedback activities. Self-evaluation encourages learners to take ownership of their learning and identify areas for improvement.

Peer Evaluation

Peer evaluation involves learners providing feedback and assessing the work of their peers. It fosters collaboration, critical thinking, and communication skills. Peer evaluation methods may include group projects, peer reviews, or collaborative assessments. Peer evaluation helps learners better understand the subject while promoting a supportive learning environment.

Evaluation of learning is a crucial aspect of instructional design and training. By employing these different types of evaluation, you can gather comprehensive data on learners' progress, identify areas for improvement, and make informed decisions to enhance the learning experience. Selecting and combining evaluation methods based on the learners' learning objectives, context, and specific needs is vital.

XI

Instructional Design for the Classroom

This section focuses on Instructional Design for the classroom, specifically for people aspiring to become instructional designers and trainers. Let's delve into the fundamental components of instructional design for the classroom and explore some suitable examples.

Needs Analysis: Before designing any instructional program, it's crucial to conduct a needs analysis to identify the gap between learners' existing knowledge and the desired learning outcomes. This analysis helps instructional designers understand the learners' characteristics, their goals, and any constraints they may face. For example, imagine a company looking to train its employees on a new software application. A needs analysis would involve assessing employees' current proficiency levels, identifying specific areas of improvement, and understanding how the training can align with their job responsibilities.

Learning Objectives: Once the needs analysis is complete, instructional designers must define clear and measurable learning objectives. Learning objectives outline what learners should be able to do or know by the end of the instruction. For instance, if the aim is to teach high school students about the water cycle, a suitable learning objective could be: "By the end of the lesson, students will be able to describe the stages of the water cycle and explain their significance."

Instructional Materials: Developing instructional materials is crucial to instructional design - selecting appropriate resources, such as textbooks, multimedia presentations, interactive activities, and assessments. Consider an example where a trainer designs a workshop on business communication skills for professionals. The instructional materials could include PowerPoint slides, case studies, role-playing exercises, and handouts that provide practical tips and techniques for improving communication.

Instructional Strategies: Choosing the right instructional strategies is essential to engaging learners and facilitating effective learning. Instructional designers should consider various methods, such as lectures, group discussions, hands-on activities, simulations, and multimedia presentations. Let's take the example of teaching mathematics to elementary school students. An instructional strategy like using manipulatives, such as counting blocks or fraction strips, can help students understand abstract concepts through hands-on experiences.

Assessment and Evaluation: Assessment and evaluation are critical components of instructional design to measure learners' progress and the effectiveness of the instruction. Assessment methods can include quizzes, tests, projects, or presentations. For example, in a training program for customer service representatives, an assessment could involve role-playing scenarios where learners demonstrate their ability to handle customer complaints effectively.

Iterative Design: Instructional design is an iterative process. It involves continuous evaluation and improvement of instructional materials and strategies based on feedback and data gathered during implementation. For instance, an instructional designer may collect feedback from learners through surveys or observations to identify areas for improvement in the learning experience.

In conclusion, instructional design is a systematic approach to designing compelling learning experiences. By conducting a needs analysis, defining learning objectives, developing appropriate instructional materials, implementing engaging instructional strategies, and evaluating the outcomes, instructional designers can create impactful learning experiences in various contexts. Remember, the examples provided are just a glimpse of the possibilities, and the applications of instructional design are numerous.

XII

Instructional Design for Training

To illustrate the concepts of instructional design for training, let's consider an example scenario:

Scenario: A large retail company approaches you to design a training program for its newly hired customer service representatives. The goal is to equip them with the knowledge and skills to provide exceptional customer service and handle various customer inquiries and issues.

Needs Analysis

- Conduct interviews and surveys with the company's stakeholders, managers, and experienced customer service representatives to identify the specific training needs.
- Analyze job descriptions and performance expectations to understand the required competencies.

Learning Objectives

Develop clear, measurable, and achievable learning objectives that align with the identified needs. Make use of Bloom's taxonomy to set learning objectives. For example, "By the end of the training, participants will be able to handle customer complaints effectively and empathetically."

Content Development

- Organize the training content into modules or units based on logical sequencing and the complexity of the topics.
- Use various instructional strategies, such as lectures, case studies, role-plays, and simulations, to cater to different learning styles and engage the participants.
- To enhance learning and retention, create visually appealing and interactive multimedia materials like videos, infographics, and interactive quizzes.

Instructional Delivery

- Determine the most suitable delivery method for the training program, such as in-person workshops, virtual classrooms, or blended learning approaches.
- Select and train competent instructors or facilitators to deliver the training effectively.
- Provide an opportunity for participants to practice and apply the newly acquired knowledge and skills through hands-on activities and real-life scenarios.

Assessment and Evaluation

- Develop formative and summative assessments to measure the participants' progress and determine the effectiveness of the training program.
- To evaluate the participants' knowledge, skills, and attitudes, use a mix of assessment methods, including quizzes, practical exercises, and observational assessments.

- Collect feedback from participants, instructors, and supervisors to identify areas for improvement and make necessary revisions to the training program.

Continuous Improvement

- Analyze the assessment and evaluation data to identify strengths and weaknesses of the training program.
- Regularly update and refine the training materials based on feedback and emerging trends in customer service.
- Stay updated on the latest instructional design theories, methodologies, and technologies to enhance the effectiveness of future training programs.

Remember, instructional design is a dynamic and iterative process that requires continuous evaluation and improvement. By following this systematic approach, instructional designers can create engaging and impactful training programs that meet learners' needs and achieve the desired learning outcomes.

XIII

Instructional Design for Distance Education

This chapter will explore the world of instructional design tailored explicitly for distance education. With the increasing demand for online learning, educators must develop effective instructional strategies that engage and empower learners in virtual environments. We will delve into the nitty-gritty of instructional design for distance education and provide suitable examples to illustrate these concepts. Let's begin!

Understanding the Learners

In distance education, it is vital to understand learners' diverse needs and characteristics. Consider factors such as their technological proficiency, learning preferences, prior knowledge, and availability of resources. For instance, if designing a book for adult learners who work full-time, using 24*7 accessible asynchronous learning materials would be beneficial. On the other hand, if the target audience consists of tech-savvy students, interactive multimedia elements enhance engagement.

Example: Imagine designing an online language book for beginner-level learners. By recognizing their limited knowledge, the instructional designer can provide interactive activities such as virtual flashcards, pronunciation exercises, and real-life dialogues to develop their language skills effectively.

Clear Learning Objectives

Well-defined learning objectives guide the instructional design process. They provide a roadmap for the book content, assessment methods, and learning outcomes. Objectives should be specific, measurable, achievable, relevant, and time-bound (SMART), ensuring that learners clearly understand what they will achieve by the end of the book.

Example: A clear learning objective in a distance education book on financial literacy could be: "By the end of this book, learners will be able to create a personal budget, identify different types of investments, and analyze financial statements."

Engaging Content and Activities

To maintain learner interest and motivation, instructional designers must create engaging content and activities incorporating multimedia elements such as videos, podcasts, infographics, and interactive simulations. They should also design collaborative activities like discussion forums, virtual group projects, and peer assessments to foster social interaction and knowledge exchange among learners.

Example: In a distance education book on environmental sustainability, the instructional designer could incorporate videos showcasing real-life examples of sustainable practices, interactive quizzes to reinforce learning and a virtual group project where learners collaborate to propose sustainable solutions for their local communities.

Effective Assessment Strategies

Assessment plays a crucial role in distance education. It not only measures learner progress but also provides valuable feedback for improvement. Use multiple assessment tools to gauge understanding. Incorporate self-assessment activities, quizzes, assignments, and project-based assessments that align with the learning objectives.

Example: In an online coding book, the instructional designer could include coding challenges with automated feedback, code review sessions, and a final project where learners showcase their programming skills.

Ongoing Evaluation and Iteration

Continuously evaluate the effectiveness of your instructional design and make necessary improvements. Gather feedback from learners through surveys, discussions, or assessments. Analyze learning analytics and usage data to identify areas that require enhancement. Regularly update content to reflect current trends and technologies.

Example: An instructional designer designing a distance education book on data analysis could review feedback from learners to identify challenging concepts and refine instructional materials accordingly. They might also update the book content to include emerging data analysis tools and techniques.

Instructional design for distance education requires a thoughtful approach to effectively engaging and supporting learners. By understanding learners' needs, setting clear objectives, creating engaging content, employing effective assessment strategies, and continuously evaluating the design, instructional designers can create meaningful and impactful learning experiences. Remember, innovation and adaptation are essential in the ever-evolving landscape of online education. Good luck on your journey to becoming exceptional instructional designers and trainers in distance education!

XIV

Instructional Design for Multimedia

In this chapter, we will explore the exciting field of instructional design for multimedia, focusing on how to create engaging and compelling learning experiences. With the increasing demand for online education fuelled by the rapid advancement of technology, multimedia plays a crucial role in capturing learners' attention and enhancing their understanding. Let's dive in and discover some critical aspects of instructional design for multimedia and look at some examples that will empower you to excel in this field.

Understanding Multimedia Instructional Design

Multimedia instructional design integrates various media elements, such as text, images, audio, video, and interactive features, to create immersive and impactful learning experiences. Here are some essential considerations:

a. Analyzing Learners: Before designing multimedia-based instruction, it's crucial to understand the target audience's characteristics, prior knowledge, and learning preferences. This analysis informs the selection and integration of multimedia elements.

b. Defining Objectives: Clear learning objectives are the foundation for effective instructional design. Define specific, measurable, achievable, relevant, and time-bound (SMART) objectives tuned to the desired learning outcomes.

c. Media Selection: Choose multimedia elements based on their ability to support the instructional goals and engage learners effectively. For example, using videos to demonstrate a complex process or incorporating interactive simulations for hands-on practice.

Strategies for Multimedia Instructional Design

Let's explore some strategies that can help you create compelling and impactful multimedia-based learning experiences:

a. Storytelling: Incorporate storytelling techniques to engage learners emotionally and enhance information retention. For example, create scenarios or case studies that allow learners to apply their knowledge in realistic contexts.

b. Visual Design: Utilize visually appealing graphics, illustrations, and diagrams to simplify complex concepts and aid comprehension. Consider using infographics, mind maps, or concept maps to represent relationships between ideas visually.

c. Interactivity: Engage learners through interactive elements such as quizzes, simulations, branching scenarios, and gamification. These elements promote active learning, critical thinking, and skill development.

d. Multimedia Integration: Combine multiple media elements synergistically to enhance learning experiences. Supplementing textual content with relevant images, audio narration, or video demonstrations can reinforce understanding.

Examples of Effective Multimedia Instructional Design

Let's look at a few examples that demonstrate how multimedia can be effectively integrated into instructional design:

a. Online Language Learning: Interactive language learning platforms often use multimedia elements like videos, audio recordings, and interactive exercises to teach vocabulary, pronunciation, and cultural aspects. These elements immerse learners in real-life situations and foster language acquisition.

b. Medical Training Simulations: Multimedia-based simulations are a boon for medical professionals who can now practice complex procedures in a controlled environment. These simulations often incorporate 3D models, videos, and interactive elements to provide a realistic and immersive learning experience.

c. Corporate Training: Multimedia is extensively used in corporate training to deliver engaging and interactive experiences. For instance, e-learning modules may include videos, infographics, and interactive scenarios to train employees on topics such as compliance, sales techniques, or leadership skills.

Incorporating multimedia elements into instructional design can transform learning experiences, making them more engaging, interactive, and effective. By understanding learners' needs, defining clear objectives, and employing effective strategies, instructional designers can create immersive multimedia-based books that promote deep understanding and skill development. Remember, as instructional designers and trainers, your role is to empower learners, and multimedia instructional design is a fantastic tool for achieving that goal.

XV
Instructional Design for e-Learning

This chapter will discuss instructional design for e-learning, a rapidly growing field that is crucial to creating compelling online learning experiences. In e-learning, instructional designers combine educational principles, technology, and multimedia elements to create engaging and interactive learning experiences.

The key steps involved in the instructional design process for e-learning are:

Needs Analysis: Before designing any e-learning content, conducting a thorough needs analysis is essential. Needs analysis involves identifying the target audience, learning goals, prior knowledge, and specific needs or constraints. For example, if the target audience is healthcare professionals learning about new medical procedures, the instructional designer must understand their existing knowledge and specific challenges.

Learning Objectives: Clearly define the desired learning outcomes or objectives of the e-learning book. Learning objectives should be specific, measurable, achievable, relevant, and time-bound (SMART). For instance, an e-learning book on project management might have educational outcomes like "learners will be able to create a project schedule using Gantt charts" or "learners will understand the different stages of project risk management."

Content Development: Based on the learning objectives, develop the core content of the e-learning book. Content development can include text-based content and multimedia elements such as videos, audio recordings, interactive exercises, quizzes, simulations, and assessments. Use various instructional strategies to cater to different learning styles and engage learners effectively. For example, a book on photography could include instructional videos demonstrating multiple techniques, followed by interactive quizzes to reinforce learning.

Instructional Strategies: Choose appropriate instructional strategies based on the content and the target audience. Examples of instructional strategies include storytelling, case studies, scenario-based learning, problem-solving activities, discussions, and collaborative projects. These strategies promote active learning and help learners apply their knowledge in real-world contexts. For instance, an e-learning book on customer service skills might include interactive scenarios where learners make decisions in simulated customer interactions.

User Interface and Experience: Pay attention to the design of the e-learning platform or Learning Management System (LMS). Ensure the user interface is intuitive, visually appealing, and easy to navigate. Consider the overall user experience, including accessibility, responsiveness across different devices, and compatibility with multiple browsers. Well-designed e-learning platforms enhance learner engagement and make the learning process smoother.

Assessment and Feedback: Include formative and summative assessments to measure learner progress and provide feedback. Formative assessments, such as quizzes or interactive exercises, help learners gauge their understanding during the learning process. Summative assessments, like end-of-book quizzes or assignments, evaluate learner achievement at the end of the book. Provide timely and constructive feedback to learners to guide their learning journey and reinforce their understanding.

Iterative Design and Evaluation: Instructional design is an iterative process, and continuously evaluating the e-learning book's effectiveness is essential. Gather feedback from learners, subject matter experts, and other stakeholders to identify areas for improvement. Use analytics and data provided by the e-learning platform to monitor learner engagement, completion rates, and performance. Revise and refine the book based on feedback and evaluation results.

Remember, effective instructional design for e-learning goes beyond simply transferring information online. It involves creating interactive and engaging content that caters to the needs of diverse learners.

Examples of successful e-learning resources designed with instructional design principles include:

1. Bookra: Bookra offers a wide range of online books from leading universities and institutions worldwide. Their books often include interactive video lectures, quizzes, and assignments, allowing learners to engage with the content actively. The books also provide opportunities for peer interaction and feedback.

2. Khan Academy: Khan Academy provides free, self-paced educational content covering various subjects. Their instructional design incorporates short video lessons, practice exercises, and progress tracking. The content is presented in a conversational and accessible style, making it suitable for learners of all ages.

3. Duolingo: Duolingo, a language learning platform, engages learners with gamification and bite-sized lessons. It incorporates interactive exercises, quizzes, and progress tracking, creating an immersive and enjoyable learning experience.

These examples demonstrate how effective instructional design principles can be applied to e-learning, resulting in engaging and impactful online learning experiences. By considering the needs of the learners, setting clear objectives, leveraging multimedia elements, and incorporating interactive strategies, instructional designers can create practical e-learning books that promote meaningful learning and learner success.

XVI
Blended Learning and Flipped Classroom Approach

Blended learning and the flipped classroom approach change how students learn and teachers teach. This chapter will explore how these methods combine traditional classroom experiences with online learning to create a more flexible and personalized education. By flipping the classroom, students can engage with content at their own pace before coming to class, where they can dive deeper into discussions and activities. This blend of learning styles not only makes education more accessible but also helps students take charge of their learning journey.

Blended Learning - The Future of Education

The world of education is evolving constantly, and Blended Learning is one of the most exciting recent developments. Blended learning refers to combining traditional classroom instruction with online learning methods. It is a flexible and dynamic approach that allows students to learn at their own pace and in their own ways. Let's explore the benefits of Blended Learning for educators and learners in today's changing world and also talk about the challenges.

Benefits of Blended Learning

Personalized and Flexible Learning

Blended learning allows trainers to offer learners the flexibility they need to manage their time effectively and control their learning journey. With a combination of offline and online education, learners can easily adjust their schedules to accommodate other responsibilities, learn at their own pace, and access learning resources that they can study outside of class. This flexibility also means learners can better manage distractions, improve focus, and retain more information.

Promotes active learning

Blended learning promotes active learning. This teaching approach encourages learners to engage more deeply with the learning material and apply what they have learned in practical situations. Blended learning environments make it easier for trainers to incorporate active learning activities such as online quizzes, group projects, and discussion forums, allowing learners to share ideas, collaborate, and engage more actively with the material. By enabling learner participation, trainers can help create learners who are more motivated, curious, and confident in their ability to apply knowledge.

Provides immediate feedback

Blended learning provides learners with immediate feedback. Trainers can use online tools, such as learning management systems, quizzes, and surveys, to monitor learners' progress. By providing instant feedback, trainers can reduce the time it takes to identify and address areas of weakness, which can significantly improve the quality of learning. Real-time feedback also helps trainers monitor the effectiveness of their teaching and adapt and modify their approach to better support specific learner needs.

Enhances learner engagement

Blended learning also enhances learner engagement. By incorporating digital resources, trainers and educators can create interactive and engaging learning experiences that cater to different learning styles and provide learners with multimedia content such as videos, animations, simulations, and quizzes. These tools motivate and inspire learners while reinforcing key concepts and skills. By keeping learners engaged, trainers can help reduce the dropout rates in their courses and ensure that the learning experience is both relevant and meaningful to learners.

Increases cost-effectiveness

Finally, blended learning can also save significantly for trainers and educators. By moving some aspects of the learning experience online, trainers can reduce the physical resources and infrastructure required for classroom-based learning, such as textbooks, handouts, and classroom space. The long-term benefits of a blended learning approach also extend to improved learning outcomes, higher levels of engagement, and the ability to cater to more learners without adding more trainers.

Challenges of Blended Learning

Preparedness of Educators

Many educators need help blending traditional teaching methods with online learning resources. For blended learning to become fully effective, it requires proper training, professional development, and an understanding of digital technology.

Technical Issues

Blended learning involves using digital devices and online platforms, which may experience connectivity issues, website downtime, or other malfunctions. Fixing such issues can be time-consuming and hamper the learners' learning experience.

Lack of Self-Discipline

Blended learning requires self-discipline and self-motivation from learners to manage their time and progress on their coursework. Lacking these qualities, a student may fall behind in completing the course.

Incorporating Blended Learning in Your Sessions

We've already discussed that blended learning combines traditional classroom teaching with online instruction, optimizing learners' time and enhancing their knowledge retention. Now, let's look at how to incorporate blended learning effectively in your sessions and deliver better outcomes for your learners.

Determine your learning objectives: Firstly, you need to determine your learning objectives - what outcomes do you want your learners to achieve? This step will enable you to choose the right blend of learning activities to achieve your desired goal. For example, if you want your learners to master a new skill, you can incorporate self-paced online modules followed by a practical classroom session.

Select the appropriate learning tools: The key to effective blended learning is to find the right mix of tools that work best for your learners. While plenty of online tools and platforms are available, you should look for the right combination that works for your learning objectives, budget, and technological capabilities. Some popular tools include learning management systems (LMS), virtual classrooms, social media, gamification, etc.

Create engaging and interactive content: As the digital landscape becomes more crowded, educators and trainers must create content that learners can connect with. The key is to make your content interactive, fun, and relevant. You can incorporate videos, quizzes, games, simulations, and case studies into your content to engage learners and keep them motivated.

Promote active learning: Active learning is a pedagogical approach emphasizing learner-centered, experiential, and collaborative learning. In a blended learning context, you can promote active learning by incorporating group discussions, peer evaluations, and collaborative projects into your session. This will encourage learners to collaborate, share knowledge, and develop critical thinking skills.

Evaluate and measure effectiveness: Finally, it's essential to evaluate and measure the effectiveness of your blended learning program. This will help you determine the gaps in your delivery and make necessary changes to enhance its effectiveness. Tools like surveys, feedback forms, and data analytics can help you measure the effectiveness of your program.

Blended learning is truly the future of education and learning, and by incorporating it into your training sessions, you can provide your learners with a richer and more engaging learning experience. From personalized learning to cost-effective education, blended learning offers numerous benefits to educators and learners alike. However, the challenges associated with it must be addressed, and educators must be trained to use digital technology for teaching. By creating an optimal blended learning environment, the learners can expect a richer, more engaging, and more effective learning experience in the future.

Flipped classroom approach

Have you ever been in a training session or classroom where the facilitator just talks and talks without engagement? If yes, you know how boring and mundane it feels.

The traditional teaching method, in which the instructor delivers lectures in the classroom, followed by assignments and assessments, is gradually shifting towards a more effective and tech-savvy approach known as the flipped classroom.

A flipped classroom is a teaching methodology in which learners watch or read the material before class and come prepared with questions and ideas they discuss with their peers in the session. The instructor assists the learners in problem-solving and inquiry-based learning in the classroom. The flipped classroom engages the learners and allows them to work at their pace while providing teachers with time to support students one-on-one.

How do you incorporate a flipped classroom approach in your sessions?

Moving away from the traditional approach is often difficult as it means leaving your comfort zone. Here are some tips to help you get started.

Understand Your Audience

Before you start incorporating a flipped classroom approach, it is essential to understand your audience or learners. Different individuals have different learning styles and preferences, such as learning through listening, reading, or visuals. Knowing the preferred learning style to design online lectures and assessments that align with your learners' needs is beneficial. You can use a survey, quiz, or assessment tool to discover your learners' learning styles. In addition, understanding your audience's demographics, including their age, culture, and language, can enhance their learning experience.

Record Your Presentations and Lessons

After understanding your learners' learning styles and preferences, the next step is to create engaging, interactive, and concise online content. Record your lessons and presentations ahead of time. This can be done through screen recordings, PowerPoint presentations, videos, diagrams, images, and audio to convey the information visually. Ensure that online materials articulate the learning objectives clearly and align with the learners' preferred learning style. You can use e-learning development tools like Articulate 360, Adobe Captivate, and Camtasia to create interactive and engaging online lectures.

Prepare Interactive Exercises Instead of Lectures

The next step is preparing interactive exercises for the classroom session. These activities include problem-solving, group work, inquiry-based and real-life scenarios, or online quizzes. By doing this, you create an engaging environment where learners apply the knowledge they learned and ask questions while collaborating with others. Interactive exercises facilitate effective knowledge retention, leading to better understanding and long-term memory retention. You can use various classroom management tools, such as Kahoot, Mentimeter, and Nearpod, to conduct active learning activities and monitor the learners' progress.

Provide Personalized Feedback

A crucial aspect of the flipped classroom approach is providing personalized feedback to learners. You can create quizzes, surveys, and formative assessments to evaluate the learners' progress and understanding. Pre-assessments can also help instructors understand the learners' prior knowledge, skills, and experiences. During the interactive sessions, pay attention to each learner's contributions and provide valuable feedback. Feedback can be through suggestions, comments, rubrics, and one-on-one interaction with learners. Personalized feedback helps learners develop critical thinking and improves their overall performance. It also shows them that their contributions are valued, leading to higher motivation.

Use Technology to Your Advantage

The flipped classroom approach heavily relies on technology. Educators can use online tools such as Google Classroom, Quizlet, or Kahoot to provide learning materials, monitor progress, and evaluate learner performance. These tools provide an interactive learning experience and help educators effectively track large classrooms. You can also use social media and online forums to create communities where students can connect and continue the conversation after class.

Evaluate and Reflect

Evaluating and reflecting on the effectiveness of the flipped classroom approach can enhance the learning experience for both the learners and instructors. Collecting feedback from the learners and reflecting on the outcomes can help identify the approach's strengths and weaknesses. You can use evaluation tools, such as surveys, feedback forms, and classroom observations, to gather feedback from learners. You can also reflect on the learners' engagement level, their performance, and the areas of improvement.

Be Prepared to Adapt and Innovate

Teaching approaches are flawed, and the flipped classroom method is no exception. As an educator, you must be prepared to adapt and innovate constantly. Take the time to assess the needs of your learners and adjust your approach accordingly. Also, remember to incorporate the suggestions of your learners. Doing so ensures that you remain relevant and provide an effective learning experience.

The flipped classroom approach is a fantastic teaching method that caters to all types of learners. It encourages meaningful engagement and facilitates effective knowledge retention, leading to better understanding and long-term memory retention. Whether you are a trainer, educator, learning and development professional, or facilitator, incorporating this approach into your sessions will transform your teaching style and positively impact your learners. With the growing availability of online tools and technology, there has never been a better time to flip your classroom.

So, go ahead and try out the flipped classroom approach in your next session, and see the difference it makes in your learners' engagement and learning outcomes.

Empowering Future Instructional Designers And Trainers

Congratulations! You have reached the end of **"Instructional Design is NOT Rocket Science."** Over the past sixteen chapters, we have delved into the fascinating world of instructional design and explored various approaches and strategies for effective teaching and training. Aspiring instructional designers and trainers like yourselves now have a grasp on the knowledge and tools to create transformative learning experiences for your future learners. It's time to reflect on key takeaways from the book and discuss the importance of continuous learning and growth in this field.

1. The Holistic Approach to Instructional Design: Throughout this book, we emphasized the importance of adopting a holistic approach to instructional design. Effective instruction goes beyond merely transmitting information; it requires understanding learners' needs, goals, and prior knowledge. By employing instructional strategies that cater to diverse learning styles, leveraging technology, and incorporating real-world applications, instructional designers and trainers can create engaging and meaningful learning experiences.

2. Learner-Centered Instruction: A learner-centered approach is one of the cornerstones of effective instructional design. The learning process is aimed at learners, and their needs and interests should guide the method of instruction. As budding instructional designers and trainers, creating a supportive and inclusive learning environment that fosters collaboration, critical thinking, and self-directed learning is essential. By incorporating formative assessments and feedback mechanisms, you can continuously monitor learners' progress and make necessary adjustments to ensure optimal learning outcomes.

3. Adapting to Technological Advancements: In today's digital era, instructional designers and trainers must be well-versed in utilizing technology as a powerful tool for learning. From learning management systems and online collaboration platforms to virtual and augmented reality, many digital resources are available to enhance instruction and create immersive learning experiences. Embrace technological advancements, stay up-to-date with emerging trends, and experiment with new tools to maximize the effectiveness of your instructional designs.

4. The Role of Reflection and Evaluation: Effective instructional design is an iterative process that requires constant reflection and evaluation. As you embark on your journey as instructional designers and trainers, remember to review and assess the effectiveness of your instructional approaches regularly. Seek feedback from learners, colleagues, and other stakeholders to identify areas for improvement and make necessary adjustments. Embracing a growth mindset and being open to continuous learning will refine your skills and deliver increasingly impactful instruction.

5. Embracing Collaboration and Professional Development: Instructional design and training are collaborative fields, and no one can thrive in isolation. Engage with professional communities, attend conferences, and participate in workshops to expand your network and exchange ideas with fellow educators. Seek mentorship opportunities and learn from experienced professionals in the field. Additionally, stay abreast of current research, educational theories, and emerging instructional practices to enhance your expertise and remain at the forefront of this sector.

As I conclude this book, I encourage you to embark on your journey as instructional designers and trainers with enthusiasm and a commitment to lifelong learning. The world of education is ever-evolving, and as professionals in this arena, you have the power to shape the future of learning. Remember, every learner is unique, and by leveraging practical instructional approaches and designing transformative learning experiences, you can profoundly transform the lives of those you teach.

Thank you for joining me in this book, and I wish you all the best in your future endeavors as instructional designers and trainers. May you inspire and empower learners to reach their full potential!

Keep learning, keep growing, and keep making a difference!

BONUS RESOURCE – GAME UP YOUR TRAINING PROGRAM

Types of Training Games and Activities

Ice-Breakers and Energizers

Use interactive session-starters or "energizers" to wake the participants and renew their focus after longer learning sessions. Ice breakers are activities that establish a connection between the participants and encourage them to engage with one another. These also help as a team-building exercise. For instance, you can try the Blindfold Obstacle game, where participants are blindfolded and paired and communicate with each other to lead through stretches that simulate obstacles and hurdles.

Role Playing

Role-playing is a great way to engage participants in a training program. Role-playing is a simulation that puts the participant in a decision-making context where one behaves like a character they are expected to play. By playing such roles, the participants learn and practice real-world scenarios and situations they might face. For example, in role-playing exercises for customer service training, participants play poser calls to learn to handle upset customers and provide ideal customer service.

Board Games

Board games or game shows are excellent learning experiences that participants enjoy. They are great for teamwork, communication, critical thinking, and problem-solving. Trainers may incorporate board games such as Business Plan Competition, which challenges the participants to form teams and create a mock business plan. Board games create a setting that provides a fun-filled environment for deeper learning.

Simulation Games

These games are digital recreations that simulate a realistic scenario that the participants might encounter in their workplace in the future. Simulations provide a risk-free environment for employees to learn complex procedures and situations. For example, a team leader in training could use a simulation game that recreates a team-building activity, mocks up the difficulties of dealing with team members, and provides guidelines for managing such a team.

Gamification

Gamification incorporates gaming elements, such as points, badges, leaderboards, or rewards, into non-gaming environments, such as training. For example, in gamification, trainers create incentives like bonuses to motivate employees to learn with a goal. Trainers may reward employees who understand and incorporate new skills into their workplace. This kind of training offers great motivation and encourages healthy competition among colleagues.

The interactivities may seem trivial to training professionals but significantly impact participants' understanding and retention. Incorporating these exercises will make your training program more engaging and the process more effective. So, prepare to "game up" your training programs while ensuring the desired, significant learning objectives.

Ice-breaker Activities

Begin the training session with ice-breaker activities, such as "Two Truths and a Lie" or "Human Bingo." These activities help participants get to know each other and create a comfortable learning environment.

1. Two Truths and a Lie:

- Each participant thinks of two true and one false statement about themselves.
- They take turns sharing these statements with the group.
- The group tries to guess which information is a lie.
- This activity encourages participants to share fun facts about themselves

and sparks conversation.

2. Human Bingo:

- Create bingo cards with different descriptions or facts in each square (e.g., "Has traveled to five countries," "Speaks more than two languages").
- Distribute the cards to participants, instruct them to find people in the group who match the descriptions, and have them sign their squares.
- The first person to fill out their bingo card yells, "Bingo!" and shares interesting facts about the people they met.

3. Name That Hobby:

- Ask each participant to share their name and one of their hobbies or interests.
- To make it more engaging, you can set a timer and limit the time for each introduction.
- As each person shares, others can take note of common interests they might share.

4. Personal Timeline:

- Provide participants with a blank paper or whiteboard sheet.
- Ask them to draw a timeline highlighting their life's key events, milestones, and achievements.
- Afterward, each participant shares their timeline with the group, explaining the significance of their chosen events.

5. Group Storytelling:

- Begin a collaborative storytelling activity where each participant contributes one sentence to create a group story.
- Go around the room, and each person adds to the story until it reaches a satisfying conclusion.
- This activity encourages creativity and cooperation.

6. Memory Sharing:

- Provide participants with a prompt related to memories, such as "Share a memorable childhood experience" or "Tell us about a recent adventure."
- Allow each person to take a few minutes to share their memory.
- Encourage active listening and ask follow-up questions.

7. Life Timeline String:

- Distribute a long piece of string or yarn to each participant.
- Instruct them to create a visual timeline of their life by placing knots or loops at specific points along the thread to represent significant life events.
- After everyone has completed their timeline, have participants share their stories while following the string.

8. Team-building Interview:

- Pair up participants and give them a few minutes to interview each other.
- Instruct them to learn about their partner's background, interests, and experiences.
- Afterward, each person introduces their partner to the group, sharing what they've learned.

9. Would You Rather:

- Present participants with a series of "Would You Rather" questions that prompt interesting choices (e.g., "Would you rather have the ability to fly or be invisible?").
- Ask each participant to choose one option and briefly explain their choice.
- This activity promotes light-hearted discussion.

10. Emoji Introduction:

- Provide participants with a list of common emojis or emoticons.
- Ask each person to select one that best represents how they feel or who they are at that moment.
- Participants then take turns explaining their choice and why they relate to that emoji.

Remember to choose ice-breaker activities appropriate for the group's size, dynamics, and time constraints. These activities foster connection, break the ice, and set a positive tone for the rest of the session.

Sales Team Training Activities

Interactive games and activities can benefit sales team training programs by engaging participants and reinforcing critical skills and concepts.

1. Role Play:

- Assign participants into pairs or small groups.
- Provide each group with a sales scenario or role-play card.
- Ask them to act out the scenario, with one participant playing the salesperson and the other playing the customer.
- Afterward, provide feedback and facilitate a discussion on what went well and what could be improved.

2. Sales Jeopardy:

- Create a Jeopardy-style game board with different categories and point values related to sales topics.
- Divide participants into teams.
- Ask teams to choose a group and point value, then present them with a sales-related question.
- If they answer correctly, they earn the points. If not, give another team the chance to respond.

3. Product Knowledge Quiz:

- Prepare a set of quiz questions related to your products or services.
- Optionally, use buzzers for a competitive element.
- Have participants answer the questions individually or in teams.
- Provide explanations for correct answers and discuss any misconceptions.

4. Sales Objection Handling:

- Create objection scenarios or cards that represent common objections.
- Pair participants and assign them different roles as salespeople and customers.
- Have the salespeople practice handling objections while the customers raise objections.
- Provide feedback and switch roles if necessary.

5. Speed Selling:

- Show participants a product or a picture of a product.
- Give them a limited time (e.g., 1-2 minutes) to pitch the product to the group.
- Encourage them to focus on key selling points and practice brevity.

6. Cold Calling Simulation:

- Provide participants with a cold calling script.
- Have them make simulated cold calls to other participants or role-playing customers.
- Review and discuss the calls, highlighting strengths and areas for improvement.

7. Negotiation Role Play:

- Create negotiation scenarios or cards with different negotiation objectives.
- Assign roles to participants (e.g., buyer and seller) and provide them with background information.
- Allow participants to negotiate while adhering to their objectives.
- Debrief and discuss negotiation strategies and outcomes.

8. Sales Pitch Contest:

- Give participants time to prepare a sales pitch for a product or service.
- Let them deliver their pitches to a panel or the entire group.
- Use a scoring system or vote to determine the winning pitch.

9. Customer Persona Matching:

- Provide participants with customer profiles and descriptions of your products or services.
- Ask them to match the customer personas with the most appropriate products or services.
- Discuss the matches and reasons behind their choices.

10. Sales Bingo:

- Create Bingo cards with sales-related terms or concepts instead of numbers.
- Distribute the cards to participants.
- Call out definitions or scenarios related to the terms, and participants mark their cards accordingly. The first to complete a row or column shouts, "Bingo!"

11. Sales Scavenger Hunt:

- Create a list of clues or questions about your products or services.
- Divide participants into teams.
- Provide the first clue or question and have teams follow the clues to find specific items or learn about your offerings.
- The first team to complete the hunt wins.

12. Price Negotiation Game:

- Prepare a list of products or services with different prices.
- Assign participants into pairs or small groups.
- Have them negotiate the price of a product, with one playing the buyer and the other the seller.
- Set a time limit for negotiations.

13. Sales Simulation Software:

- Invest in or use specialized sales simulation software or platforms.
- Provide participants access to the software to engage in realistic sales scenarios.
- Monitor and provide feedback based on their performance.

14. Sales Strategy Board Game:

- Acquire a sales board game like "The Sales Game."
- Organize teams and have them play the board game, which simulates sales challenges and decisions.
- Encourage discussion about strategies and outcomes.

15. Elevator Pitch Practice:

- Set a timer for one minute.
- Have participants take turns delivering a concise elevator pitch for a product or service.
- Provide feedback on clarity and impact.

16. Customer Feedback Analysis:

- Provide participants with customer feedback data.
- Ask them to analyze the feedback to identify common trends, areas for improvement, and customer preferences.
- Encourage discussions on how to address the feedback.

17. Sales Storytelling Workshop:

- Present examples of successful sales stories.
- Provide participants with storytelling prompts related to your products or services.
- Have participants create and share their sales stories, focusing on engaging narratives.

18. Competitive Analysis Game:

- Share competitor profiles and market research data with participants.
- Divide them into teams and ask each team to analyze a specific competitor.
- Have teams present their findings and discuss implications for your sales strategy.

19. Sales Role Swap:

- Assign participants to different roles within the sales process (e.g., lead generation, prospecting, closing).
- Allow them to experience and appreciate the challenges and responsibilities of each role.
- Discuss insights gained from the role swap.

20. Sales Pitch Roulette:

- Write down different sales topics or scenarios on paper and place them in a hat.
- Participants take turns drawing topics and delivering impromptu sales pitches on the chosen topics.
- Encourage creativity and adaptability.

21. Customer Journey Mapping:

- Provide participants with customer journey templates or diagrams.
- Guide them in mapping out a customer's typical journey, from awareness to purchase.
- Discuss touchpoints and opportunities for improvement.

22. Sales Team Quiz Show:

- Set up a quiz show format with a host or facilitator.
- Include sales-related questions in various categories.
- Divide trainees into teams and have them compete by answering questions using buzzers.

23. Sales Goal Setting:

- Distribute goal-setting worksheets to participants.
- Guide them in setting specific, measurable, achievable, relevant, and time-bound (SMART) sales goals.
- Encourage them to track progress over time.

24. Sales Presentation Peer Review:

- Assign participants to create sales presentations on a specific topic.

- Have them deliver presentations to the group.
- After each presentation, allow for peer feedback and constructive criticism.

25. Sales Pitch Video Analysis:

- Provide participants with recording equipment or smartphones.
- Ask them to record their sales pitches.
- Review the recorded pitches as a group, highlighting strengths and areas for improvement.

26. ROI Calculator Workshop:

- Provide participants with ROI calculators and case studies.
- Teach them how to calculate ROI for your products or services.
- Have them apply the concept to real-life scenarios.

27. Cross-Selling and Upselling Simulation:

- Create scenarios where participants must identify opportunities for cross-selling or upselling.
- Encourage them to propose additional products or services to customers in various scenarios.

28. Customer Testimonial Creation:

- Provide video recording equipment and scripts.
- Ask participants to create video testimonials as if they were satisfied customers.
- Discuss what makes a credible customer testimonial.

29. Sales Ethics Discussion:

- Present ethical dilemmas related to sales.
- Facilitate a group discussion on ethical considerations in sales, including honesty, transparency, and customer trust.

30. Gamified Sales Training Apps:

- Identify and use gamified sales training apps designed for skill-building and learning.
- Encourage participants to explore and engage with these apps independently or in groups.

Adapt these activities to your specific training goals and ensure that each session includes debriefing and discussion to reinforce learning and encourage reflection.

Customer Service Training Activities

Customer service training programs can benefit from interactive games and activities as well.

1. Role Play:

- Divide participants into pairs or small groups.
- Provide each group with a customer service scenario or role-play card.
- Ask them to act out the scenario, with one participant playing the customer and the other the customer service representative.
- Afterward, provide feedback and facilitate a discussion on what went well and what could be improved.

2. Customer Service Scenarios Quiz:

- Prepare quiz questions based on various customer service scenarios and challenges.
- Optionally, use buzzers for added engagement.
- Have participants answer the questions individually or in teams.
- Provide explanations for correct answers and discuss best practices for handling similar situations.

3. Product Knowledge Relay:

- Create teams and set up a relay race format.
- Prepare product information sheets for different products or services your team supports.

- Each team member must share product knowledge before handing the baton to the next team member.
- The team that completes the relay with the most accurate and comprehensive product knowledge wins.

4. Complaint Resolution Challenge:

- Provide participants with a list of sample customer complaints or issues.
- Ask each participant or team to choose one complaint to work on.
- Challenge them to find creative and rational solutions to resolve the complaints.
- Have participants present their answers to the group for discussion and feedback.

5. Service Recovery Simulation:

- Create customer service scenarios that involve service failures or dissatisfied customers.
- Assign roles to participants as customers and customer service representatives.
- Participants must practice service recovery techniques to turn unhappy customers into satisfied ones.
- After each scenario, facilitate a discussion on what worked and what could be improved.

6. Customer Feedback Analysis:

- Provide participants with customer feedback data, such as surveys or comments.
- Ask them to analyze the feedback to identify common issues, trends, and areas for improvement.
- Encourage participants to create action plans based on the input to address identified issues.

7. Customer Persona Matching:

- Prepare customer profiles or personas that represent different customer segments.

- Provide descriptions of your products or services.
- Ask participants to match the customer personas with the products and services that best fulfill their needs.
- Discuss the matches and reasons for their choices, emphasizing the importance of understanding customer profiles.

8. Empathy Building Exercise:

- Use empathy-building exercises or scenarios to help participants practice understanding and connecting with customers on an emotional level.
- Provide scenarios that evoke various emotions or challenges.
- Motivate participants to share their feelings about each scenario and discuss how empathy can be applied in customer interactions.

9. Live Chat Simulation:

- Utilize live chat simulation software or platforms.
- Assign participants to play the roles of customer service representatives and customers.
- Participants engage in simulated live chat interactions, focusing on typing speed, accuracy, and providing helpful responses.
- After each simulation, review the chat logs and discuss improvements.

10. Customer Journey Mapping:

- Distribute customer journey templates or diagrams to participants.
- Guide them collaboratively in mapping the typical customer journey - from the first contact to post-purchase support.
- Encourage discussions about key touchpoints and opportunities for better service at each stage.

11. Mystery Shopper Scenarios:

- Assign participants roles as mystery shoppers and customers.
- Create mystery shopper scenarios that include specific evaluation criteria.
- Ask the mystery shoppers to evaluate the customer service provided by their colleagues based on the scenarios.

- Collect feedback and scores to discuss areas of improvement.

12. Complaint Role Play:

- Prepare a list of complaint scenarios or role-play cards.
- Divide participants into pairs or small groups.
- Have one participant act as the customer with a complaint while the other plays the customer service representative.
- Participants must practice handling the complaint effectively and professionally.
- After each role-play, provide feedback and switch roles.

13. Communication Skills Workshop:

- Conduct workshops on various communication skills, including active listening, effective communication, and conflict resolution.
- Use role-play scenarios to allow participants to practice and apply these skills.
- Provide guidance and constructive feedback during and after the role-play exercises.

14. Service Standards Challenge:

- Share your company's customer service standards and guidelines with participants.
- Create customer service scenarios that require participants to apply these standards.
- Challenge them to identify how specific standards should be applied in different situations.
- Discuss their responses and guide aligning with service standards.

15. Handling Difficult Customers Game:

- Create cards describing complex customer profiles or personas.
- Distribute the cards to participants and ask them to brainstorm strategies for handling each demanding customer.
- Encourage participants to share their insights and best practices for managing challenging customer interactions.

16. Customer Service Storytelling:

- Present examples of compelling customer service stories or anecdotes.
- Provide storytelling prompts related to customer service scenarios.
- Have participants create and share customer service stories, focusing on engaging narratives and positive outcomes.

17. Positive Language Exercise:

- Provide participants with lists of positive and negative language examples.
- Challenge them to rewrite negative customer responses or statements more positively and more customer-friendly.
- Discuss the significance of using positive language in customer interactions.

18. Conflict Resolution Role Play:

- Prepare conflict scenarios or role-play cards that involve customer disputes.
- Assign roles to participants, with one participant playing the customer and the other the customer service representative.
- Participants must practice conflict resolution techniques and de-escalation.
- After each role-play, provide feedback and discuss effective conflict resolution strategies.

19. Customer Service Scenario Cards:

- Create scenario cards with customer service situations, challenges, or dilemmas.
- Distribute the cards to participants or teams.
- Ask participants to discuss and analyze the scenarios, applying their knowledge and problem-solving skills to identify the best action.

20. Service Excellence Awards:

- Recognize outstanding customer service behaviors and achievements

within the team.
- Present awards or certificates to exemplary team members who consistently demonstrate exceptional customer service skills.
- Celebrate and share success stories with the entire team to inspire others.

21. Cross-Departmental Training:

- Collaborate with other departments within your organization to exchange knowledge and insights.
- Invite guest speakers or trainers from other departments to share their expertise with your customer service team.
- Foster a culture of cross-functional learning and understanding.

22. Customer Service Trivia:

- Organize a trivia game with questions about customer service practices, policies, and company values.
- Divide participants into teams and encourage friendly competition.
- Provide explanations for correct answers and use the game to reinforce important information.

23. Customer Service Ethics Discussion:

- Present ethical dilemma scenarios related to customer service interactions.
- Facilitate discussions about ethical considerations in customer service, including honesty, privacy, and fairness.
- Encourage participants to share their perspectives and ethical guidelines.

24. Customer Service Feedback Surveys:

- Share customer feedback survey results with participants.
- Analyze and discuss the feedback to identify areas where customer service can be improved.
- Encourage participants to brainstorm and implement action plans based on customer feedback.

25. Complaint Handling Workshop:

- Conduct workshops on effective complaint-handling techniques.
- Provide participants with complaint handling guidelines, scripts, and role-play scenarios.
- Allow participants to practice handling customer complaints and resolving issues.
- Offer feedback and discuss strategies for improving complaint resolution skills.

26. Time Management Exercise:

- Challenge participants to complete customer service tasks within specified time limits.
- Provide a list of timed tasks or scenarios that simulate real-time customer interactions.
- Emphasize the importance of efficiency and time management in providing prompt and effective service.

27. Multichannel Customer Service Simulation:

- Create scenarios that involve customer interactions through various channels, such as phone, email, live chat, and social media.
- Assign participants to engage with customers across different channels and practice delivering consistent and high-quality service.
- Discuss the unique challenges and best practices for each channel.

28. Service Recovery Game:

- Create a game where participants must select the most appropriate service recovery response for different scenarios.
- Use response cards with potential actions or responses.
- Encourage participants to contemplate the impact of their choices on customer satisfaction and loyalty.

29. Social Media Customer Service Simulation:

- Simulate customer interactions on social media platforms, including responding to inquiries, addressing complaints, and providing information.

- Provide guidelines for effective social media customer service.
- Review participants' responses and discuss the importance of maintaining a professional online presence.

30. Gamified Customer Service Training Apps:

- Utilize gamified apps and platforms for customer service training.
- Encourage participants to explore these apps independently or in a group setting.
- Monitor progress and performance within the app to track skill development.

Customize these activities to align with your training goals and the customer service team's unique challenges. Encourage open discussion, role-play, and constructive feedback to reinforce learning and improve customer service skills.

❦

Leadership Development Training Activities

Leadership development training programs can benefit from interactive games and activities that help participants enhance their leadership abilities.

1. Leadership Role Play:

- Divide participants into pairs or small groups.
- Provide each group with a leadership scenario or role-play card.
- Ask them to act out the script, with one participant taking on the leadership role.
- Afterward, have participants provide feedback and facilitate a discussion on leadership behaviors and styles.

2. Leadership Styles Quiz:

- Administer participants a leadership style assessment (e.g., transformational, servant, autocratic).
- Discuss the results and their implications for leadership.

- Encourage participants to explore different leadership styles and their applications in various situations.

3. Trust-fall Challenge:

- Pair the participants with similar physical attributes, e.g., height, weight, etc.
- Discuss the concept of trust and open communication.
- Ask the partners to stand in two lines with one partner's back towards the other.
- At the whistle, the partners in front will fall back, and the partners behind them will catch them.
- Reverse the positions of partners and repeat.
- Facilitate discussion on how easy or difficult it was to trust their partners.

4. Leadership Strengths and Weaknesses Analysis:

- Provide participants with assessment tools to identify their leadership strengths and weaknesses.
- Encourage self-reflection and discussion about how to leverage strengths and address weaknesses in leadership roles.

5. Vision Statement Workshop:

- Download and share vision statement templates with the participants.
- Guide participants in crafting a vision statement for their leadership roles or teams.
- Discuss the importance of a clear and inspiring vision in leadership.
- Allow participants to present their vision statements and offer feedback.

6. Leadership Storytelling:

- Provide storytelling prompts related to leadership challenges or successes.
- Teach participants the art of leadership storytelling by demonstrating.
- Have participants create their leadership stories that inspire and convey essential leadership lessons.

- Encourage participants to narrate their stories to the group.

7. Decision-Making Simulation:

- Present participants with decision-making scenarios that leaders commonly face.
- Encourage them to make decisions, discuss their reasoning, and evaluate the outcomes.
- Use decision matrices to analyze the decision-making process.

8. Leadership Ethics Discussion:

- Discuss ethical considerations in leadership, including integrity, fairness, and transparency.
- Present ethical dilemma scenarios.
- Encourage participants to share their insights and solutions.

9. Leadership Book Club:

- Ask the participants to name/quote their favourite leadership book or article.
- Encourage them to write one leadership principle from the book or article that they found useful.
- Initiate discussion on applying the principles they learned to their leadership roles and key takeaways.

10. Leadership TED Talk Analysis:

- Select TED Talk videos featuring leadership topics or speakers.
- Watch the videos as a group.
- Facilitate discussions on key insights, strategies, and takeaways.
- Encourage participants to share how they think they'll apply the lessons to their leadership roles.

11. Leadership Development Plan:

- Provide participants with templates to create individual leadership development plans.

- Guide them in setting specific leadership goals and action steps to achieve them.
- Encourage regular progress reviews and adjustments.

12. Leadership Case Studies:

- Analyze leadership case studies or real-life examples of successful and challenging leadership situations.
- Encourage participants to identify leadership principles and strategies used in each case.
- Discuss lessons learned.

13. Leadership Strengths-Based Workshop:

- Administer strengths assessment tools to participants.
- Encourage them to explore and leverage their strengths in their leadership roles.
- Discuss how they can apply their strong suit to improve team dynamics and achieve goals.

14. Leadership Podcast Discussions:

- Select leadership-related podcast episodes for participants to listen to independently.
- Organize group discussions to share insights and reflections from the podcasts.
- Explore how podcast content can be applied to leadership challenges.

15. Leadership Feedback Exchange:

- Pair participants and have them exchange feedback on each other's leadership behaviors and styles.
- Encourage constructive and specific feedback.
- Guide how to use feedback for growth and improvement.

16. Change Management Simulation:

- Simulate change management scenarios and challenge participants to

lead their teams through change.
- Discuss different change management models and strategies.
- Evaluate the effectiveness of leadership during the change process.

17. Leadership Quotes Analysis:

- Share inspirational leadership quotes with participants.
- Have them analyze the quotes and discuss their relevance to leadership principles and behaviors.
- Encourage participants to share their favorite leadership quotes and explain why they resonate with them.

18. Emotional Intelligence (EQ) Assessment:

- Administer EQ assessments to participants to measure their emotional intelligence.
- Discuss the importance of EQ in leadership.
- Explore strategies for developing EQ competencies.

19. Conflict Resolution Role Play:

- Organize role-play scenarios that involve leadership in conflict resolution.
- Assign roles to participants, with one playing the leader and the other involved in the conflict.
- Encourage leaders to practice effective conflict resolution strategies.

20. Leadership 360-Degree Feedback:

- Implement a 360-degree feedback process where leaders receive feedback from peers, subordinates, and superiors.
- Analyze the feedback together.
- Identify areas for leadership improvement and development.

21. Mentoring Program:

- Establish a mentoring program where experienced leaders mentor less experienced ones.

- Ask mentors to help mentees set and achieve leadership goals.
- Encourage mentors to share their leadership experiences and provide guidance on improvement.

22. Leadership Competency Assessment:

- Present a leadership competency framework to participants.
- Ask them to self-assess their competency levels in various leadership areas.
- Create action plans to develop competencies where improvement is needed.

23. Leadership in Crisis Simulation:

- Simulate crises that require strong leadership.
- Assign participants leadership roles to manage the situation.
- Evaluate their crisis management decisions and strategies.
- Discuss lessons learned.

24. Leadership Feedback Circles:

- Form small groups of participants who regularly provide and receive feedback on their leadership behaviors and challenges.
- Encourage a safe and supportive environment for open and honest discussions.
- Ask participants to share their experience of delivering and receiving feedback.

25. Leadership Bookshelf:

- Create a leadership bookshelf with a selection of leadership books.
- Assign different books to participants.
- Give them time to read (this could be overnight or days, depending on the length of the training program).
- Host discussions on significant takeaways, insights, and applications to leadership roles.

26. Leadership Podcast Production:

- Have participants work in teams to plan and produce leadership-focused podcast episodes.
- Each team can choose a leadership topic and interview experts or discuss leadership challenges.
- Share the podcast episodes within the group and organization.

27. Leadership Networking Events:

- Organize leadership networking events or forums where leaders from different departments or organizations can connect and share experiences.
- Provide structured discussion topics to facilitate meaningful conversations.

28. Leadership Retreat:

- Plan a leadership retreat or off-site event.
- Encourage participants to engage in team-building activities, leadership workshops, and self-reflection.
- Create a supportive and inspiring environment for leadership development.

29. Leadership Action Learning Projects:

- Assign leadership action learning projects that challenge participants to apply leadership principles to real-world situations.
- Participants can work individually or in teams to tackle leadership-related challenges.
- Encourage the participants to share their experience of working in a team and how effectively they managed the challenge.

30. Leadership Mindfulness and Well-being Session/Workshop:

- Conduct a session/workshop on leadership mindfulness and well-being.
- Teach participants mindfulness techniques to reduce stress, enhance focus, and promote well-being.
- Discuss the connection between well-being and effective leadership.

Customize these activities to suit your specific leadership development goals and the needs of your participants. Encourage open discussions, self-reflection, and ongoing feedback to foster leadership growth and improvement.

෩

Soft Skills Training Activities

In today's rapidly evolving world, professional and personal development hinges on technical expertise and robust soft skills. These interpersonal, communication, and emotional intelligence skills are the building blocks of success, helping individuals navigate the complexities of the modern workplace and fostering rewarding personal relationships.

The Role of Games and Activities in Soft Skills Training:

Games and activities are powerful tools for developing soft skills for several reasons. Games and interactive activities capture participants' attention and make learning enjoyable. This engagement enhances the retention and application of soft skills. Experiential learning allows individuals to practice soft skills in a safe and controlled environment, helping build confidence and competence.

Games and activities often include feedback mechanisms that facilitate self-awareness and improvement. Trainees can see the impact of their soft skills on outcomes. Many games simulate real-life scenarios, making it easier for participants to transfer their learning to practical situations. Team-based games foster collaboration, communication, and trust among participants, strengthening their interpersonal skills. Games can help individuals recognize and manage their emotions, a fundamental component of emotional intelligence.

Incorporating games and activities into your soft skills training program is about making learning fun and creating a compelling and memorable learning experience. By mastering essential soft skills through interactive and engaging methods, individuals can unlock their full potential professionally and personally and thrive in an ever-changing world.

This section will examine various games and activities focusing on these essential soft skills.

Active Listening Activities:

1. **Listening Pairs:**

- Pair up participants and have one person share a personal story or experience while the other listens attentively without interrupting.
- Afterward, the listener summarizes what they heard, and the speaker confirms if it was accurate.
- Then, switch roles.

2. **Active Listening Trios:**

- In groups of three, one person is the speaker, one is the active listener, and the third is the observer.
- The observer provides feedback on the listener's active listening skills while the speaker shares a story or information.
- Rotate roles for each round.

3. **Listening Circle:**

- Arrange participants in a circle.
- One person starts by sharing a brief personal story or experience.
- The person to their left must then summarize the story accurately.
- Continue around the circle, with each person summarizing the story they heard.

4. **Mindful Listening Meditation:**

- Guide participants through a mindful listening meditation.
- Play soothing music or nature sounds.
- Instruct participants to focus solely on the sounds, practicing deep listening without judgment or distraction.

5. **Listening to Music:**

- Play instrumental music or a song with meaningful lyrics.
- Ask participants to close their eyes and listen actively to the music.
- Afterward, facilitate a discussion about their emotional responses and interpretations.

6. **Emotion Charades:**

- Prepare cards with different emotions written on them (e.g., happy, sad, angry).
- Each participant draws a card and expresses the emotion through body language and facial expressions while others guess the emotion being portrayed.
- This activity helps participants become more attuned to non-verbal cues.

7. **Active Listening Role Play:**

- Create scenarios that involve active listening, such as a customer complaint or a colleague seeking advice.
- Pair participants and assign roles as the speaker and the active listener.
- Participants practice active listening skills, including asking clarifying questions and providing empathetic responses.

8. **Silent Partner Drawing:**

- Pair participants and give one person a simple drawing to describe without showing it to their partner.
- The partner listens actively and tries to recreate the drawing based solely on the verbal description.
- Afterward, compare the pictures to emphasize the importance of clear communication.

9. **Storytelling with a Twist:**

- In a group, one person starts a story with a single sentence.
- The next person adds a sentence, and so on, with each participant contributing to the story.
- However, there's a catch: participants must listen carefully to previous contributions to maintain coherence.

10. Listening Reflection Journal:

- Encourage participants to keep a listening reflection journal.
- After each interaction or conversation, they write down their thoughts on the effectiveness of their active listening skills.
- Ask them to include what went well and what they can improve.

Effective Communication Activities:

1. Communication Styles Quiz:

- Administer a communication styles quiz to participants.
- Ask them to identify their communication preferences (e.g., assertive, passive, aggressive).
- Discuss the different styles and their impact on interactions.

2. Feedback Sandwich:

- Pair participants and have one person provide constructive feedback to the other.
- However, they must structure their feedback like a sandwich, starting with a positive comment, then constructive feedback, and ending with another positive observation.
- Later, ask them to share their experience and guide them on improvements (choice of words, tone, etc.).

3. Listening and Responding:

- Divide the group in pairs.
- One person shares a personal experience or opinion in pairs while the other listens carefully.
- After the speaker finishes, the listener must respond with a statement that validates the speaker's feelings or perspective.
- This activity emphasizes empathetic and validating communication.

4. Non-verbal Communication Charades:

- Prepare cards with non-verbal cues or body language expressions (e.g., crossed arms, nodding).
- Ask participants to draw a card one by one.
- The person drawing the card will express the non-verbal cue without using words.
- The group guesses the expression being portrayed.

5. **Clear Instructions Challenge:**

- Provide participants with written instructions for a simple task.
- The challenge is for them to convey the instructions to a partner orally without showing the written instructions.
- The partner must then complete the assignment based on the oral instructions.
- Discuss any challenges faced, highlighting the importance of clear communication.

6. **Debate and Persuasion:**

- Organize a debate on a relevant topic.
- Assign participants to teams with opposing viewpoints.
- Each team must prepare arguments and counterarguments, practicing persuasive communication skills.
- After the debate, facilitate a discussion on effective persuasion techniques.

7. **Role Reversal:**

- Pair participants and assign each pair a communication scenario (e.g., job interview, negotiation).
- Initially, one person plays the role of the effective communicator, while the other plays the role of the ineffective communicator.
- Afterward, they switch roles and discuss the differences in communication.

8. **Active Listening and Clarification:**

- Provide participants with a list of statements that require clarification

due to ambiguity or vagueness.
- Participants take turns reading a statement and ask clarifying questions.
- This activity enhances both active listening and clarification skills.

9. Empathy Building Through Art:

- Ask participants to create artwork (e.g., drawings, collages) that reflect the emotions or experiences of someone they've recently interacted with.
- This artistic expression helps participants develop empathy by seeing things from another's perspective.

10. Communication Styles Simulation:

- Assign participants roles with different communication styles (e.g., passive, assertive, aggressive).
- Present a communication scenario (e.g., conflict resolution).
- Participants must role-play the scenario while embodying their assigned communication style.
- This will allow them to explore the impact of different communication styles on interactions.

These activities can be adapted and combined to create engaging and comprehensive training programs for active listening and effective communication. Encourage participants to reflect on their communication skills and implement what they learn in real-world scenarios.

Time Management Activities:

1. The Pomodoro Technique:

- Introduce participants to the Pomodoro Technique - a time management approach that involves working in focused intervals of usually 25-30 minutes followed by short breaks.
- Allocate individual tasks to each participant.
- Have participants apply this technique to the task they must complete during the training session.
- In the end, discuss the challenges faced by participants.

2. Time Blocking Exercise:

- Provide participants with a daily schedule template.
- Ask them to make a list of their daily tasks.
- Now, participants need to time-block their day, allocating specific time slots for different tasks and activities.
- Discuss effective time-blocking strategies and the benefits of this approach.

3. Task Priority Matrix:

- Share a matrix with four quadrants labeled "Urgent and Important," "Urgent but Not Important," "Important but Not Urgent," and "Neither Urgent nor Important."
- Participants list their tasks in the appropriate quadrant.
- This helps them prioritize their workload.

4. Delegate and Prioritize Game:

- In a group, present a set of tasks or scenarios that individuals do daily.
- Now, the participants take turns deciding whether to delegate, tackle immediately, or schedule for later based on priority.
- Discuss the decision-making process and the importance of delegation.

5. Time Tracking Challenge:

- Ask participants to track their time for a day or a week, recording how they spend each hour.
- Analyze the data as a group to identify time wasters and opportunities for better time management.

6. Deadline Juggling:

- Create a game where participants receive a set of tasks with different deadlines.
- They must strategize and plan how to meet all the deadlines effectively.
- This activity helps develop time management and planning skills.

7. Time Management Role Play:

- Assign participants roles in a work scenario that requires effective time management.
- They must prioritize tasks, delegate when necessary, and manage their time to complete the scenario successfully.
- Debrief on time management strategies.

8. Multitasking vs. Single-tasking Experiment:

- Divide participants into two groups.
- One group is tasked with multitasking, while the other focuses on single-tasking.
- Compare the results to highlight the advantages of single-tasking in terms of productivity and reduced stress.

9. Time Management Simulation Game:

- Create a time management simulation game where participants manage a virtual calendar, scheduling appointments, tasks, and personal time.
- Participants must make choices to optimize their schedules and achieve their goals.
- Facilitate discussion on what challenges they faced.

10. Time Management Tips Exchange:

- Ask participants to share their favorite time management tips and techniques with the group. Create a collaborative list of time management strategies.
- Share these as PDFs or PowerPoint presentations that participants can refer to and implement in their daily routines.

Stress Management Activities:

1. Deep Breathing Exercise:

- Start the session with a deep breathing exercise.

- Instruct participants to sit comfortably, close their eyes, and take slow, deep breaths for a few minutes.
- This helps participants relax and focus.

2. **Stress Ball Workshop:**

- Provide participants with stress balls.
- You can also DIY stress ball materials (e.g., balloons and rice).
- Guide them in making stress balls and explain how they can use them as stress-relief tools during tense moments.

3. **Stressor Identification Activity:**

- Ask participants to identify and list personal and professional life stressors.
- Encourage open discussion about triggers and stressors.
- Explore strategies to manage them, ask participants to share what works best for them.

4. **Progressive Muscle Relaxation:**

- Lead participants through a progressive muscle relaxation exercise.
- Instruct them to tense and then relax each muscle group, focusing on releasing tension and stress.

5. **Stress Journaling:**

- Provide participants with stress journals or notebooks.
- Encourage them to journal daily about their stressors, emotions, and coping strategies. Participants should review their journal entries periodically to identify patterns and areas for improvement.

6. **Mindfulness Meditation:**

- Guide participants through a mindfulness meditation session.
- Encourage them to be present in the moment, focusing on their breath and sensations.
- Discuss the benefits of regular mindfulness practice for stress reduction.

7. Stress Reduction Role Play:

- Assign participants roles in stressful workplace scenarios, such as conflicts or tight deadlines.
- Have them role-play these scenarios while applying stress reduction techniques, such as deep breathing or assertive communication.
- Facilitate discussion on what worked and what didn't.

8. Stress Management Action Plan:

- Ask participants to create personalized stress management action plans.
- They should identify their stressors, list coping strategies, and set specific goals for managing stress effectively.
- Facilitate discussion so that participants can share their coping strategies.

9. Laughter Yoga:

- Engage participants in yoga exercises involving playful laughter and deep breathing.
- Laughter yoga can boost mood and reduce stress.
- Lead them through a series of laughter-inducing activities.

10. Stress Ball Toss:

- Provide participants with stress balls or soft objects.
- Create a circle, and participants take turns sharing a stressor they've experienced before tossing the ball to another participant.
- The receiver offers a brief encouragement or empathy before sharing their stressor.

These activities help participants develop practical skills for managing their time more effectively and reducing stress. Encourage participants to implement the techniques they learn daily for lasting benefits.

Negotiation Skills Activities:

1. Role-Play Negotiation:

- Assign participants roles in a negotiation scenario, such as a salary negotiation or a business deal.
- Encourage them to practice negotiation techniques, including active listening, compromise, and finding mutually beneficial solutions.
- Discuss how easy or difficult they found to reach an amicable solution.

2. **The Trading Game:**

- Provide participants with items with an assigned value.
- Ask them to trade with each other to maximize the total value of their possessions.
- At the end, each participant will be asked to calculate the value of their items.
- This game teaches the principles of value creation in negotiation.

3. **Win-Win Negotiation:**

- Present a negotiation scenario where both parties can benefit.
- Discuss and demonstrate the importance of seeking win-win outcomes rather than zero-sum situations.
- Ask participants to practice creative problem-solving and compromise.

4. **Negotiation Styles Workshop:**

- Introduce different negotiation styles, such as competitive, collaborative, and accommodating.
- Assign participants a negotiation style and have them practice negotiating with others with different styles.
- Encourage the participants to explore the pros and cons of each technique.

5. **Negotiation Poker:**

- Distribute poker chips to participants and share business scenarios requiring negotiation.
- Like a traditional poker game, participants negotiate with each other using poker chips as bargaining tools.
- They must make strategic decisions about when to fold, raise, or call,

thereby learning negotiation tactics.

6. Cross-Cultural Negotiation Simulation:

- Create a negotiation scenario that involves cultural differences.
- Assign participants roles in the negotiation and provide information about their assigned culture's cultural norms and expectations.
- Encourage participants to practice cross-cultural negotiation skills.
- Facilitate post-activity discussion so participants can share the ease or difficulty they faced.

7. Negotiation Debriefing:

- This activity follows a negotiation role-play or a real-life negotiation experience-sharing session.
- Conduct a debriefing session.
- Discuss what went well, what could be improved, and the primary negotiation strategies employed.

8. Mock Sales Pitch:

- Assign participants roles as buyers and sellers in a sales pitch scenario.
- Participants practice negotiation skills as they haggle over the terms of a sale.
- Emphasize the importance of building rapport and finding common ground.

9. Conflict Resolution Role Play:

- Organize role-play scenarios involving conflicts, such as a workplace disagreement or a customer complaint.
- Assign participants roles and ask them to practice conflict resolution strategies.
- The focus should be on de-escalation and finding mutually agreeable solutions.

10. Negotiation Skills Reflection:

- Divide participants into small groups.
- Provide each group with negotiation case studies or real-life examples and ask them to analyze them.
- After analyzing the cases, participants reflect on the negotiation techniques, outcomes, and what they would do differently.

Decision-Making Activities:

1. **Decision-Making Styles Assessment:**

- Have participants complete a decision-making styles assessment to identify their preferred decision-making approach (e.g., intuitive, analytical, consensus-based).
- Discuss the different styles and their strengths and weaknesses.
- Encourage participants to share which style works for them and which doesn't.

2. **Decision-Making Case Studies:**

- Provide participants with decision-making case studies or scenarios.
- Ask them to analyze the situations, identify key decision points, and recommend courses of action.
- Encourage discussions on decision-making criteria and risk assessment.

3. **The Dice Game:**

- Create a situation game where participants must decide based on the dice roll.
- Assign outcomes to different dice rolls.
- Divide participants into groups.
- Each group will roll the dice on their turn and discuss the decision-making process under uncertainty.

4. **Decision-Making Simulation:**

- Develop a decision-making simulation game with multiple rounds.
- Divide participants into small groups.

- When faced with a situation, the group must make choices and face consequences based on that choice.
- The group is allowed to adjust their decisions based on outcome or feedback.
- This activity teaches adaptive decision-making.

5. **The Pros and Cons Matrix:**

- Ask participants to make a significant personal or professional decision.
- Have them create a pros and cons matrix to assess the advantages and disadvantages of different options.
- You can also ask them to do a SWOT analysis of their decision.
- This structured approach helps participants weigh their choices.

6. **Decision-Making Role Play:**

- Divide participants into groups.
- Give each group a decision-making scenario, such as a board meeting or a crisis response team.
- Assign participants roles in decision-making scenarios.
- They must collaborate and make decisions as a team, considering various perspectives and viewpoints.

7. **Ethical Dilemma Discussion:**

- Present ethical dilemmas related to the participants' field or industry.
- Ask participants to make choices, individually or in groups.
- Encourage discussions about the ethical considerations involved in decision-making and how to make moral choices.

8. **Decision Tree Analysis:**

- Teach participants how to create decision trees to map out complex decisions visually.
- Provide scenarios and ask participants to build decision trees to evaluate potential outcomes and alternatives.
- This activity is best carried out individually.

9. **The 2-Minute Drill:**

- Challenge participants to make quick decisions in a time-pressured environment.
- Present them with rapid-fire scenarios and ask for their immediate choices.
- You can conduct this activity individually or in groups.
- This activity enhances decision-making under time constraints.

10. **Decision-Making Journal:**

- Encourage participants to keep a journal.
- After each significant decision, they record their thought process, factors considered, and the outcome.
- Regularly reviewing their diary helps improve decision-making skills over time.

These activities help participants develop effective negotiation and decision-making skills while providing opportunities for practice, reflection, and learning from successes and challenges.

Conflict Resolution Activities:

1. **Role-Play Conflict Scenarios:**

- Create scenarios involving conflicts, such as workplace disagreements or interpersonal disputes.
- Assign participants roles in the scenarios.
- Ask them to practice conflict resolution techniques, including active listening, empathy, and problem-solving.

2. **Conflict Resolution Cards:**

- Develop conflict resolution cards with common conflict scenarios on one side and suggested resolution strategies on the other.
- In groups or pairs, participants draw cards and discuss how to apply the approach to each scenario.
- Discuss the reasoning behind that approach and whether a different

approach would better suit the scenario.

3. **Mediation Simulation:**

- Set up a mediation simulation where participants are disputing parties and a mediator.
- Participants must work together to find a resolution.
- The mediator facilitates the process and encourages open communication.

4. **Constructive Feedback Exercise:**

- Pair participants and ask one to provide the other with constructive feedback on a specific topic or skill.
- The feedback giver should use the "I" statement technique to express their observations and feelings.
- Afterward, switch roles.
- Encourage discussion on how easy or difficult it was to give and receive feedback.

5. **Conflict Resolution Role Reversal:**

- Present a conflict scenario and assign participants to be disputing parties in groups.
- Initially, one group plays the role of the assertive communicator, while the other plays the role of the passive communicator.
- Afterward, they switch roles.
- Discuss the differences in communication.

6. **The Conflict Resolution Challenge:**

- Create a competition-style challenge where participants are presented with conflict scenarios.
- They must collaboratively find solutions.
- Award them points for effective resolution strategies and teamwork.
- Reveal scores and discuss the approach of the group receiving the highest score.

7. **Fishbowl Exercise:**

- Arrange participants in a circle (the "fishbowl").
- Select a pair to sit in the center and act out a conflict scenario while the rest of the group observes.
- Afterward, the observers discuss what they observed and suggest alternative resolution strategies.

8. **Group Conflict Resolution Simulation:**

- Present a complex group conflict scenario (e.g., project team disagreements).
- Participants work in teams to identify the conflict's root causes and propose resolution strategies.
- Each team presents its recommendations to the larger group.

9. **Conflict Resolution Bingo:**

- Create bingo cards with conflict resolution techniques or phrases in each square.
- Participants mark off squares as they hear others use these techniques during discussions or role-plays.
- This game can be played throughout the training program.
- The participant with the maximum number of techniques/phrases ticked on their card is declared the winner.

10. **Conflict Resolution Reflection Journal:**

- Encourage participants to keep a conflict resolution reflection journal.
- After each conflict experience, they record their thoughts, emotions, and strategies deployed.
- Ask them to periodically review the journal entries to identify areas for improvement.

Change Management Activities:

1. **Change Simulation Game:**

- Develop a change management simulation game where participants must navigate a series of organizational changes like an office relocation or department merger.
- Divide the participants into groups and assign roles.
- Participants, including change leaders and employees, must act according to their roles and work through the challenges of managing and adapting to change.
- Facilitate discussion on how smoothly or roughly each group's change management process went.

2. Change Impact Assessment:

- Present a hypothetical change initiative to participants.
- In small groups, participants assess the potential impact of the change on various aspects of the organization, such as processes, culture, and employees.
- Discuss the findings as a group.

3. Change Management Role Play:

- Divide participants into groups in a change management scenario, such as introducing a new technology system or a restructuring effort.
- Assign the roles of change leaders, employees, and stakeholders.
- Each group needs to address concerns and manage resistance.
- After completion of the activity, reverse the roles.
- Discuss different approaches and techniques used by groups.

4. Change Readiness Surveys:

- Provide participants with change readiness surveys or assessments.
- Ask them to complete the surveys individually and discuss the results in groups.
- Explore strategies for enhancing change readiness.

5. Change Storytelling Workshop:

- Conduct a workshop on change storytelling.
- Participants learn to craft compelling narratives that communicate the

purpose and benefits of a change initiative.
- Each participant creates their own change story and shares it with the group.

6. Change Resistance Simulation:

- Create a scenario where participants must identify and address resistance to change.
- They take on the roles of change leaders and employees and practice strategies for mitigating resistance and gaining buy-in.
- Afterward, the roles are reversed.

7. Change Impact Mapping:

- Provide participants with a visual map of the organization's current and desired future state after a change.
- Participants identify the critical changes required and the potential impacts on different stakeholders.

8. Change Communication Workshop:

- Conduct a workshop on effective change communication.
- Participants learn to develop communication plans, including key messages, channels, and timing.
- They create communication plans for hypothetical change initiatives.

9. Change Management Board Game:

- Design a board game where participants must make decisions related to change management.
- The game includes scenarios, challenges, and decision points that mirror real-life change initiatives.
- This game can be played in groups or individually, depending on the batch size.

10. Change Impact Interviews:

- Assign participants roles as change leaders and employees.

- Conduct mock interviews where employees express their concerns, questions, and feedback about a proposed change.
- Change leaders practice active listening and addressing concerns effectively.

These activities help participants develop valuable conflict resolution and change management skills while providing practical experience in handling real-life situations. Encourage participants to apply these skills in their workplaces to promote a positive and adaptable organizational culture.

Empathy Building Activities:

1. Empathy Circle:

- Arrange participants in a circle.
- One person shares a personal experience or emotion, and the others reflect on what they heard without judgment or offering solutions.
- This activity promotes active listening and empathetic responses.

2. Empathy Interview:

- Pair participants and assign one person as the interviewer and the other as the interviewee.
- The interviewee shares a personal experience or feeling while the interviewer asks open-ended questions to explore and better understand the emotions involved.
- Discuss the ease and/or difficulty from the perspectives of the interviewer and interviewee.

3. Empathy Storytelling:

- Ask participants to share personal stories highlighting moments when they felt empathy, or someone showed kindness toward them.
- Encourage reflection on the impact of compassion in those situations.

4. Empathy Cards:

- Create empathy cards with different emotions or scenarios.
- Participants draw cards and share their thoughts, feelings, and responses to the emotions or situations on the cards.
- This encourages empathy for various experiences.

5. **Role Reversal Exercise:**

- In pairs, participants share a recent challenging experience.
- Afterward, they switch roles and must articulate how they believe the other person felt during the event.
- This activity helps participants see situations from different perspectives.

6. **Empathy Art:**

- Provide art supplies to the participants.
- Ask them to create artwork (paintings, drawings, collages) that represent the emotions or experiences of others.
- This activity helps them showcase their ability to empathize and express empathy through art.
- Display this artwork across the training room or venue.
- Conducting this activity at the start of the session or on day 1 of the training program is advisable.

7. **Empathy Letter Writing:**

- Ask participants to think of someone they've had a conflict for years.
- Ask them to write empathy letters to that person.
- The notes focus on understanding the other person's perspective, acknowledging their feelings, and expressing empathy and forgiveness.
- Discuss how easy or difficult it was to express their emotions in words and forgive or seek forgiveness.

8. **Empathy Walk:**

- Conduct a silent group walk in a natural setting.
- Participants are encouraged to observe and connect with their surroundings.

- This activity will help foster a sense of empathy toward the environment and the living beings within it.

9. Empathy Book Club:

- Choose books or stories exploring themes of empathy and emotional understanding.
- Ask the participants to read the selected material. They can do this overnight.
- Facilitate discussion about the characters' experiences and the lessons learned about compassion.

10. Empathy Reflection Journal:

- Encourage participants to keep an empathy reflection journal.
- After each interaction or empathetic experience, they write down their thoughts, feelings, and insights about empathy, helping them build a habit of humane reflection.

Emotional Intelligence Activities:

1. Emotion Charades:

- Prepare cards with various emotions or facial expressions.
- Participants take turns drawing a card and expressing their emotions through facial expressions and body language.
- This activity helps in promoting emotional recognition and expression.

2. Emotion Wheel:

- Provide participants with an emotion wheel that lists a range of emotions.
- Ask each participant to roll a dice and see which emotion it lands on.
- Encourage them to identify and share times when they've felt that emotion and discuss how they managed or expressed it.

3. Emotion Matching Game:

- Create a card game with pairs of cards, each featuring an emotion word on one card and an image or description of an emotion on the other.
- Participants take turns matching the emotion word with the corresponding image or description.

4. Emotion Role Play:

- Assign participants various emotional scenarios (e.g., receiving good news, dealing with a demanding customer).
- They must act out the scenarios while trying to convey the emotions realistically.
- Afterward, discuss their experiences and observations.

5. Emotion Journal:

- Provide participants with journals and ask them to record their emotions throughout the day.
- Encourage them to describe the situations that triggered each feeling and reflect on their responses.

6. Emotion Flashcards:

- Create flashcards with different emotions written on them.
- Participants draw a card and share a personal experience related to that emotion, fostering self-awareness and emotional expression.

7. Emotion Wheel of Fortune:

- Design a game resembling "Wheel of Fortune."
- Participants spin the wheel and discuss the emotional situation or scenario they land on.
- They explore the causes, effects, and coping strategies for each scenario.

8. Emotional Intelligence Reflection:

- Initiate a group discussion or activity focused on emotional intelligence.
- Ask participants to individually reflect on how they can apply what they've learned personally or professionally.

9. Emotional Intelligence Role Model Sharing:

- Ask participants to identify and share stories of individuals they consider emotionally intelligent role models.
- They discuss the qualities and behaviours that make these individuals stand out in emotional intelligence.
- Encourage them to reflect on what qualities or behaviours they need to inculcate.

10. Emotional Intelligence Quizzes:

- Administer quizzes or assessments related to emotional intelligence, such as the EQ-i 2.0 or the MSCEIT.
- Participants review their results and identify areas for improvement.
- Discuss strategies for enhancing their emotional intelligence.

Cultural Sensitivity Activities:

1. Cultural Iceberg Activity:

- Present participants with an "iceberg" diagram in which the tip represents visible aspects of culture (e.g., clothing, food), and the submerged part portrays deeper cultural elements (e.g., values, beliefs).
- Discuss the importance of understanding cultural nuances beneath the surface.

2. Cultural Storytelling:

- Ask participants to share personal stories or anecdotes about cultural experiences, traditions, or encounters with people from diverse backgrounds.
- This activity encourages cultural sharing and understanding.

3. Cultural Sensitivity Scenarios:

- Provide scenarios that involve cultural misunderstandings or conflicts.
- Participants analyze the scenarios and identify cultural differences

individually.

- Afterward they brainstorm effective ways to address and resolve the situations as a group.

4. **Cultural Sensitivity Role Play:**

- Assign participants roles in cultural sensitivity scenarios, such as a cross-cultural business negotiation or a multicultural team meeting.
- Give them time to research on the culture of the person they'll be interacting with.
- They must practice active listening, open-mindedness, and effective communication to navigate the scenarios.

5. **Cultural Sensitivity Quiz Show:**

- Organize a quiz show-style game with questions about different cultures, customs, and traditions.
- Participants form teams and compete to answer questions, promoting cultural knowledge and awareness.

6. **Cultural Sensitivity Gallery Walk:**

- Create a "gallery" with posters or displays representing various cultures, including information about traditions, holidays, and customs.
- Participants take a gallery walk to explore and learn about different cultures.

7. **Cultural Sensitivity Reflection Circles:**

- Form small discussion circles and provide participants with prompts related to cultural sensitivity.
- They take turns sharing their thoughts and experiences while others listen empathetically.

8. **Cultural Sensitivity Simulation:**

- Develop a simulation that places participants in a multicultural environment, such as a diverse workplace or a community event.

- Participants interact with each other while practicing cultural sensitivity and adapting to different norms.

9. Cultural Sensitivity Case Studies:

- Present case studies involving cross-cultural challenges or opportunities in a workplace or community setting.
- Participants analyze the cases, identify cultural factors, and propose solutions that promote cultural sensitivity.

10. Cultural Sensitivity Action Plan:

- Encourage participants to create personalized cultural sensitivity action plans.
- They reflect on their biases, stereotypes, and areas for improvement in cultural sensitivity and outline steps to take in their daily lives to become more culturally sensitive.

These activities help participants develop empathy, emotional intelligence, and cultural sensitivity by providing experiential learning and reflection opportunities. Encourage participants to apply these skills in diverse settings to foster understanding and positive relationships.

Empowerment and Motivation Training Activities

1. Vision Board Creation:

- Help participants visualize their goals and dreams.
- Provide magazines, scissors, glue, and large sheets of paper.
- Ask participants to create a vision board by cutting out images and words representing their goals and aspirations.
- Encourage them to share and explain their vision boards with the group.
- This activity helps participants visualize their goals and dreams.

2. Affirmation Cards

- Provide index cards and art supplies.
- Ask participants to write positive affirmations or motivational quotes on

the cards.
- They can decorate them as well.
- Each person should share their affirmation and discuss how it makes them feel.
- This activity helps boost self-esteem and motivation.

3. Storytelling Circle

- Create a circle and have each participant share a personal success story about empowerment or motivation.
- Encourage active listening and ask follow-up questions to deepen the discussion.
- This activity helps encourage self-expression and shared experiences.

4. Strengths Assessment

- Provide a strengths assessment tool (like the VIA Survey of Character Strengths).
- Participants should complete the assessment and discuss their top strengths, how they can utilize them, and how those strengths empower them.
- This activity helps participants identify their strengths.

5. Goal-Setting Workshop

- Explain the SMART (Specific, Measurable, Achievable, Relevant, Time-bound) goal-setting framework.
- Ask participants to set a personal or professional goal using this method.
- Encourage them to share it with the group for feedback.
- This activity teaches effective goal-setting techniques.

6. Positive Feedback Exchange

- Pair up participants and ask them to give each other specific, positive feedback.
- Rotate partners after a few minutes.
- Encourage them to mention strengths and achievements.
- This helps foster a culture of appreciation and motivation.

7. Empowerment Through Failure

- Share stories of famous failures (e.g., Thomas Edison) and discuss how failure can lead to success.
- Ask participants to share their experiences with failure and how it eventually empowered them.
- This activity helps in changing the perspective on failure.

8. Group Mindfulness Meditation

- Lead a guided mindfulness meditation session.
- Use deep breathing exercises and encourage participants to focus on the present moment.
- Afterward, discuss how mindfulness can empower them.
- This activity helps promote self-awareness and stress reduction.

9. Role Reversal

- Have participants pair up and take turns sharing a challenge they face.
- Then, ask them to role-play, with each person taking the other's perspective.
- Afterward, discuss insights gained from the exercise.
- This activity encourages empathy and understanding.

10. Empowerment Charades

- Create a list of empowering words, phrases, or concepts related to motivation.
- Have participants take turns acting out these concepts while the others guess.
- After each round, discuss how the concepts relate to empowerment.
- This activity encourages creativity and self-expression.

11. Goal Visualization

- Guide participants through a visualization exercise where they vividly imagine achieving their goals.
- Encourage them to describe the sights, sounds, and feelings associated

with success.

- This activity helps participants mentally prepare for success.

12. Team Building Challenge

- Organize a group challenge or problem-solving activity.
- Encourage participants to work together, communicate effectively, and motivate each other to complete the task successfully.
- This helps build teamwork and mutual motivation.

13. Self-Reflection Journaling

- Provide journals or notebooks.
- Ask participants to spend time each day journaling about their experiences and feelings related to empowerment and motivation.
- Share insights and reflections as a group.
- This promotes self-awareness and personal growth.

14. Gratitude Circle

- Form a circle and have each participant share something they are grateful for.
- Continue around the circle and encourage everyone to contribute.
- Discuss how practicing gratitude can boost motivation and empowerment.
- This helps cultivate a positive mindset.

15. Empowerment Action Plan

- Have participants create a concrete action plan for achieving one of their goals.
- Encourage them to break it down into small, actionable steps with deadlines.
- Share and discuss these plans for accountability and support.
- This activity helps participants turn motivation into action.

Remember to adapt these activities to the specific needs and goals of your empowerment and motivation training workshop. Encourage open discussion and participation to maximize the impact of these exercises.

References

Berkeley Graduate Division, Teaching Guide for GSIs https://gsi.berkeley.edu/gsi-guide-contents/learning-theory-research/learning-overview/

Brown, A. L., and J. C. Campione. 1990. "Communities of Learning and Thinking, or a Context by Any Other Name." In Developmental Perspectives on Teaching and Learning Thinking Skills, ed. D. Kuhn, 108–26. Basel: Karger.

Bruner, J. S. 1960/1977. The Process of Education. Cambridge, MA: Harvard University Press.

Bruner, J. S. 1986. Actual Minds, Possible Worlds. Cambridge, MA: Harvard University Press.

Clark, R. E., & Salomon, G. (1986). Media in teaching. In M. C. Wittrock (Ed.), Handbook of research on teaching (3rd ed.). New York: Macmillan

Dewey, J. 1902/1956. The Child and the Curriculum. Chicago: University of Chicago Press.

Dewey, J. 1988. "How We Think: A Restatement of the Relation of Reflective Thinking to the Educative Process." In John Dewey: The Later Works, 1925–1953, vol. 4, The Quest for Certainty, ed. J. A. Boyston, 105–342. Carbondale: Southern Illinois University Press.

Educational Design, UNSW https://www.teaching.unsw.edu.au/educational-design

Gagné, R., & Merrill, M. (1990). Integrative goals for instructional design. Educational Technology Research & Development, 38 (1), 23-30.

Gardner, H. 1983. Frames of Mind: The Theory of Multiple Intelligences. New York: Basic Books.

Glaser, R., and E. Silver. 1994. "Assessment, Testing, and Instruction: Retrospect and Prospect." In Review of Research in Education 20, ed. L. Darling-Hammond, 393– 422. Washington, DC: American Educational Research Association.

Inhelder, B., & Piaget, J. (1958). The growth of logical thinking. New York: Basic Books.

Kagan, S. 1985. Cooperative Learning Resources for Teachers. Riverside, CA: University of California at Riverside.

Kagan, S. 1993. "The Structural Approach to Cooperative Learning." In Cooperative Learning: A Response to Linguistic and Cultural Diversity, ed. D.

D. Holt, 9–19. McHenry, IL, and Washington, DC: Delta Systems and Center for Applied Linguistics.

Newman, F., and L. Holzman. 1993. Lev Vygotsky: Revolutionary Scientist. New York: Routledge.

Schmidt, W. H., D. Jorde, L. S. Cogan, E. Barrier, I. Gonzalo, U. Moser, K. Shimizu, T. Sawada, G. A. Valverde, C. McKnight, R. S. Prawat, D. E. Wiley, S. A. Raizen, E. D. Britton, and R. G. Wolfe. 1996. Characterizing Pedagogical Flow: An Investigation of Mathematics and Science Teaching in Six Countries. Dordrecht, the Netherlands: Kluwer Academic Publishers

Teaching Guidance, The University of Queensland, Australia https://itali.uq.edu.au/teaching-guidance

Teaching Resources, Center for Teaching Innovation, Cornell University https://teaching.cornell.edu/teaching-resources

Teaching Strategies, Center for Research on Learning and Teaching, University of Michigan https://crlt.umich.edu/resources/teaching-strategies

Theories of Education, CliffNotes https://www.cliffsnotes.com/study-guides/sociology/education/theories-of-education

Thompson, P, (2019), *Foundations of Educational Technology*, Oklahoma State University Libraries, https://doi.org/https://doi.org/10.22488

Tobin, K., and D. Tippins. 1993. "Constructivism as a Referent for Teaching and Learning." In The Practice of Constructivism in Science Education, ed. K. Tobin, 3–21. Hillsdale, NJ: Erlbaum.

Vygotsky, L. S. 1978. Mind in Society: The Development of Higher Psychological Processes. Cambridge, MA: Harvard University Press.

Vygotsky, L. S. 1981. "The Genesis of Higher Mental Functions." In The Concept of Activity in Soviet Psychology, ed. J. V. Wertsch, 144–88. New York: M. E. Sharpe.

Zeichner, K. M., and S. E. Noffke. 2001. "Practitioner Research." In Handbook of Research on Teaching, 4th ed., ed. V. Richardson, 298–330. Washington, DC: Macmillan.

Zhou, Molly and Brown, David, "Educational Learning Theories: 2nd Edition" (2015). Education Open Textbooks. 1. https://oer.galileo.usg.edu/education-textbooks/1